Julia M. Eckert (ed.)
The Bureaucratic Production of Difference

Culture and Social Practice

Julia M. Eckert, professor of political anthropology at the University of Bern, explores the relation between moral norms and legal change with a particular focus on changing institutions of responsibility, liability, and redistribution. She connects these with current contestations over democratic representation, participation, security, and citizenship.

Julia M. Eckert (ed.)
The Bureaucratic Production of Difference
Ethos and Ethics in Migration Administrations

[transcript]

The publication was made possible by generous funding by the Swiss National Science Foundation

Bibliographic information published by the Deutsche Nationalbibliothek
The Deutsche Nationalbibliothek lists this publication in the Deutsche Nationalbibliografie; detailed bibliographic data are available in the Internet at http://dnb.d-nb.de

This work is licensed under the Creative Commons Attribution 4.0 (BY) license, which means that the text may be be remixed, transformed and built upon and be copied and redistributed in any medium or format even commercially, provided credit is given to the author. For details go to http://creativecommons.org/licenses/by/4.0/
Creative Commons license terms for re-use do not apply to any content (such as graphs, figures, photos, excerpts, etc.) not original to the Open Access publication and further permission may be required from the rights holder. The obligation to research and clear permission lies solely with the party re-using the material.

First published in 2020 by transcript Verlag, Bielefeld
© Julia M. Eckert (ed.)

All rights reserved. No part of this book may be reprinted or reproduced or utilized in any form or by any electronic, mechanical, or other means, now known or hereafter invented, including photocopying and recording, or in any information storage or retrieval system, without permission in writing from the publisher.

Cover layout: Maria Arndt, Bielefeld
Cover illustration: Jonathan Miaz
Proofread by Greame Currie and David Loher
Typeset by Francisco Bragança, Bielefeld
Printed by Majuskel Medienproduktion GmbH, Wetzlar
Print-ISBN 978-3-8376-5104-1
PDF-ISBN 978-3-8394-5104-5
https://doi.org/10.14361/9783839451045

Contents

The Office
Ethos and Ethics in Migration Bureaucracies[1]
Julia Eckert 7

Keeping Numbers Low in the Name of Fairness
Ethos and Ethics in a Swiss Asylum Administration
Laura Affolter 27

The Asylum Procedure in Border Detention
The Technicalities and Morals of Truth Determination in France
Chowra Makaremi 59

Moral Economy and Knowledge Production in a Security Bureaucracy
The Case of the German Office for the Protection of the Constitution
Werner Schiffauer 85

Governing the Boundaries of the Commonwealth
The Case of So-Called Assisted Voluntary Return Migration
David Loher 113

Functional Inconsistencies
State Inspection of Agricultural Labour in Switzerland
Simon Affolter 135

The Economy of Detainability
Theorizing Migrant Detention
Nicholas De Genova 155

Authors 175

The Office
Ethos and Ethics in Migration Bureaucracies[1]

Julia Eckert

What do they think they're doing?

All the contributions to this book engage with this particular question. Following the intricate analyses of what bureaucrats do,[2] we now wish to consider what they *think* they're doing. While their answers might be inter-

---

[1] The research underlying this article was made possible by a generous fellowship at the Kulturwissenschaftliche Kolleg Konstanz. I would like to thank all those participating in the discussions of the bureaucracy group at the KuKo for the insights and inspiration I gained from our conversations, namely Arthur Benz, Pascale Cancik, Mirko Göpfert, Thomas Groß, Hans Christian Röhl, Christian Rosser and Marcus Twellmann. I would also like to thank Werner Schiffauer for many inspiring discussions about states and their knowledge practices. I am grateful to Olaf Zenker, David Loher, Simon Affolter, Simone Marti, Laura Affolter and Raphael Rey for our productive discussions on bureaucratic practice. Last but not least, I would like to express my gratitude to the participants in the workshop "Ethos and Ethics in Migration Bureaucracies" that took place in September 2015 (just as Angela Merkel opened Germany's borders to refugees) for inspiring our conversation on that occasion, particularly those whose insightful contributions are not part of this publication, namely Heath Cabot, Fiorenza Picozza and Anna Tuckett.

[2] Rather than "bureaucracy", it might be better to speak of "administration", as the term bureaucracy is often used in the context of criticism. (I am grateful to Pascale Cancik for alerting me to this with her wonderful historical research on the subject. See Cancik 2004.) As we noted, people never call themselves bureaucrats. Instead, they employ terms such as civil servant, state servant, state official and social worker. The use of bureaucracy as a term of criticism alerts us to deliberations of the value of different types of skills and knowledge, the aloofness attributed to law and knowledge of procedures, contrasted with "knowledge of reality". At the same time, the reliance on references to "legality" or procedural correctness and consistency provide an insight into competing scales of value. This question of terminology is not merely a matter of the self-denomination of officials, but also the search for an appropriate analytical term that might encompass the open bound-

preted as neutralisation strategies – ex post justifications for actions that are shaped by a myriad of concerns – we hold that tracing what bureaucrats think they are doing is worthwhile for two reasons. First, we believe that what they think they *should* do shapes what they actually do as much as other constraints, whether this concerns their efforts (successful or unsuccessful) to act in what they consider an ideal manner or the formation of rationales for diverging from ideal behaviour. Second, we claim that their thinking is shaped by notions of the "office", i.e., the duties and obligations of an administration related to specific political projects. Exploring what bureaucrats *think* they do tells us about the delineation and definition of the moral community that a bureaucratic apparatus is concerned with.

To explore what *they* think they do, we employ the concept of ethics as the basis for investigating the value rationality of bureaucratic practice and its normative orientations. We see a lacuna of research on ethics in bureaucracy. Recent critiques of bureaucracy have focussed on the instrumental rationalities of bureaucratic practice, considered its orientation towards extra-bureaucratic normative demands, or posited that bureaucracies are fundamentally amoral in character (Bauman 1989; Graeber 2015; Herzfeld 1992). While some critics have attended to the wider ideological frames within which "anethical" bureaucracies are embedded, and, as in the case of Michael Herzfeld, explored the effects of an anethical role on affects (indifference or aversion), most have not examined the ways in which an ideological frame is (re-)produced in the specific narratives, categorisations and normative orientations that shape bureaucratic practice. One could say that they have fallen victim to an inflated Weberian image of rational legal rule that considers ethics and bureaucracy to be antithetical, and restricted their critical impetus to this horizon. These critiques echo early criticisms of bureaucracy, which actually coined the term (Cancik 2004), by caricaturing bureaucrats as "automatons" that stick to the rules, the letter of the law, and are indifferent towards and ignorant of the world's true problems.

Other studies of civil servants have examined the various concerns and normative orientations that shape bureaucratic practice, be it career orien-

---

aries of state administrative services. Such services often include organisations paid for by the state, but not staffed by civil servants employed by the state, to perform tasks that are interrelated with state administrative services. This also includes "civil society" organisations that are funded independently, but form part of the institutional assemblage around issues defined by state administrative concerns, such as "refugees".

tation; intra-administrative competition; extra-administrative obligations towards kin, neighbours or dependants; or simple economic interests. This laudable attention to the multiplicity of concerns that shape the practice of civil servants has introduced diversity to the image of the bureaucrat as a rule-following automaton and brought to the fore the multifarious normative orders that civil servants often operate within. What has disappeared from view, however, is how the practice of civil servants might be shaped by ideas of their "office", their "volitional allegiance" (Gill 2009: 215) to their entrusted tasks (see also Bierschenk 2014: 237-238). The ethics of office generates a specific notion of the commonweal, which structures the proper application of rules in bureaucratic practice. I use the term "commonweal" to signal a confluence between a vision of community and the goods that a community shares in. It encompasses both "commonwealth" and "common good". Neglect of this dimension of normative bureaucratic orientation has been detrimental to our understanding of how particular ideological projects, inherent in specific delineations of the commonweal, are actually translated and produced in administrative practice.

Here, we propose that ethics are intrinsic to bureaucracy. This does not make bureaucracy "good", "benevolent" or "democratic", as Du Gay (2000) suggests. Our notion of ethics is empirical (see also Fassin 2012: 4), not normative. To understand how "rule following" works, we need to attend to the ethics of office, because bureaucratic ethics defines how a specific idea of the commonweal is served. It delineates moral communities composed of those abiding in the common good from others who are excluded. In order to understand how certain political projects of specific governmentalities are put in place, we must heed the ethos and ethics at play at specific historical points in the administrative apparatus.

Contributions to this volume follow what Wedel et al. (2005: 34) suggested were a necessary focus of anthropological research on policies, namely "understanding the cultures and worldviews of those policy professionals and decision makers who seek to implement and maintain their particular vision of the world through their policies and decisions". To overcome the individualist bent often implicit in analyses of bureaucratic discretion, which might be entailed in the examination of personal worldviews, we go further by linking such worldviews to notions of "the office", and focusing on relations among political projects entailed in specific notions of the commonweal, understandings of professional roles and bureaucratic practice.³ Such professional worldviews are shaped by the structural position of particular offices at specific moments, and their designated roles within a hierarchy of offices are geared towards maintaining the good of the commonwealth.

Our aim is thus twofold. First, we introduce the notion of ethics in order to argue against the stereotype of the bureaucratic automaton, which does not account for the way normative frameworks impact on administrative conduct. Second, we address bureaucratic ethics as a means of overcoming the individualistic bent in examinations of bureaucratic discretion, and relocating the duty or obligation of the "officium" in particular relations of domination in particular historical situations.

Our analyses centre on migration bureaucracies. Here, the production and management of categories of difference, which delineate the right to partake in the commonweal, are particularly visible. All bureaucratic agencies engage in differentiating and delineating the eligibility of access to goods and services and participation in decision-making. Migration bureaucracies are not specific in this regard, but in the contemporary world of nation states where the "right to have rights" (Arendt 1968: 177) is dependent on citizenship status, they distinguish most clearly between who can partake in the commonweal and who cannot. "In contrast to other bureaucracies, (return) migration bureaucracies govern utopian social orders not through the governance of a common good, but through the shaping of the community itself," as David Loher writes in this volume. More than a territorial line separating two polities, borders differentiate access to the rights and goods within a polity. They define the moral community with which a bureaucratic ethic is concerned. Inasmuch as borders differentiate access, migration bureaucracies comprise all state agencies involved in such an endeavour. We hold that, through their work, migration bureaucracies actually produce these borders (see also De Genova 2016). A vast array of different agencies engage in delineating differential access to the specific services they administer among citizens, various categories of legal migrants and the equally numerous categories of illegalised migrants. It is not as though the assemblage of administrative actors managing differential access to rights

---

3 Heyman has earlier engaged with what he calls the "thought-work" of bureaucrats and held that "observations on thought [...] can be used to characterize the society, polity, and economy that have produced specific 'thinking situations'" (1995: 264).

and resources is a coherent and coordinated apparatus; instead, practices in these diverse "bureaus" are shaped by the diverse bio-political or disciplinary efforts they are tasked with. As they follow specific goals and logics, they are shaped by their specific role in serving the commonweal as it is defined at a particular place and time.

Such matters of definition and interpretation are intrinsic to bureaucratic work, as they establish how a specific bureaucratic agency can best serve the commonweal. We are concerned here with more than merely an extra-bureaucratic, ethical definition of the commonweal, as has often been proposed. Rather, narration, interpretation, contestation and affirmation define and interpret the commonweal in relation to the specific tasks an agency performs, and also determine who legitimately shares in the common good. Thus, close attention to ethos and ethics in the orientation of civil servants can elucidate changing understandings of the commonweal, and articulate shifting delineations between legitimate members and those defined as illegitimate.

Bringing ethics back in (to the study of the state)

Ethos and ethics: Both terms go back to Weber. For bureaucracy, only the bureaucratic ethos seems to have survived in our academic memory. But Weber distinguished between the two terms. Ethos denotes the assemblage of values that underpin procedures, such as, for example, rule orientation, consistency, efficiency, efficacy, equality before the law and depersonalisation. Today we often include transparency, and participation. Weber had a particular assemblage in mind when delineating his ideal type of rational-legal rule. We might consider this a historically specific snapshot of the values supposedly underpinning bureaucratic procedures that shaped his ideal type, albeit one that corresponds surprisingly often with bureaucrats' descriptions of what and how they want to be (Affolter 2016; Eckert 2005; Lentz 2014), and what so often they know they are not. Whatever its heuristic worth, the ideal type is frequently a standard against which civil servants measure their duties, goals and failures: it shapes expectations, claims and demands, evaluations, disappointments and resistances.

Such assemblages are specific to a time and place. The relevance of transparency today makes this clear. Entering bureaucratic ethos only in the late

20th century, transparency is not relevant everywhere to the same degree, not in each bureaucratic sector (where, e.g. street-level bureaucracies vs. pure desk jobs, or output-oriented bureaucracies vs. accounting, etc. might differ), nor in each institutional system. At least formally at specific times and places, different agencies probably share some of the values of their procedures, i.e. elements of their ethos (but see Olivier de Sardan (2009) on the role of practical norms).

Ethics, on the other hand, concerns orientation towards "the good". In the case of bureaucratic ethics, values and norms associated with the substantive goals of a bureaucratic apparatus are geared towards ideas of a good society, a good life, welfare or justice.[4] State bureaucracies, as one specific type of bureaucratic assemblage, do not merely execute bureaucratic procedures. Rather, they embrace a purpose, a *raison d'etre*, whether we actually observe a common conception of this purpose, or see several conflicting ones. Such purposes entail an ethical core (Du Gay 2000; Osborne 1994: 302). Goals and projects attributed to "the state" at a historical moment by bureaucrats, citizens and subjects alike relate to the notion of a public, a commonweal. "Their legitimacy rests on claims made manifest in a constitutional agreement and they exist for the public good," as Laura Bear and Nayanika Mathur claim (2015: 18).[5] State standards and norms are pragmatic conventions that also express notions of justice. They articulate theories of a just social order: what categories of people are eligible to benefit from what service, how much is allotted to whom, what is subsidised, what is taxed, and what can be bequeathed, etc. all relate to specific notions of justice. Bureaucratic ethics concerns each and every administrative act that declares a specific vision of social order to be "just" or "proper". In fact, the bureaucratic term for justice might be adequacy: proper, justifiable, appropriate. If conditions are appropriate to standardised needs, average situations, the proper relations of a commonweal are established.

The extent of the commonweal with which a particular bureaucratic apparatus is concerned depends on the jurisdiction of the agency in question and its degree of integration into the larger bureaucratic structure. Precisely

---

[4] This distinction between ethos and ethics corresponds to Weber's definition of both; see Swedberg 2005.

[5] Bear and Mathur use the term the "public good". I prefer to use the term "commonweal" to distinguish it clearly from a much narrower notion of "public goods".

because bureaucracies are bound to their jurisdiction, inclusion and exclusion are intrinsic to any bureaucratic work (see also Handelman 1981). Jurisdiction introduces the "nationalistic logic" that Michael Herzfeld pointed to, which serves to "distinguish between those included and excluded from the national order and to represent these distinctions as given by nature – rather than cultural or historical contingencies" (Herzfeld 1992: 174). The reformulation of jurisdiction as a *moral community* is what matters here. This reformulation, i.e. the moralization of jurisdiction, is currently prevalent in national notions of commonweal and arises from the intrinsically ethical character of any conception of a "good order". Whether someone or something deserves moral regard is shaped by norms implicit in the notion of a "good order" that a specific vision of commonweal asserts. The substantive content of visions of good order, of "the common good", introduces hierarchisation that differentiates those needing protection and support from those considered detrimental or even dangerous to maintaining the commonweal. Common good (*Gemeinwohl*) is not identical to commonwealth (*Gemeinwesen*).

How the public good is imagined, how the commonweal is conceptualised, and how those defined as outside the commonweal's moral community are treated is a matter for enquiry. The general purpose of serving the common good is made manifest in the practices, expectations, claims and disappointments related to such service. Bureaucratic ethics – like any other ethics – concerns questions of how to act in the service of these values. Thus, ethics is intrinsic to bureaucratic institutional assemblages, not merely external to them.

Often, the ethics of bureaucratic practice have been perceived to arise from extra-bureaucratic social realms, and conflict with the bureaucratic ethos as caused precisely by an incompatibility between the ethical and social realm and the rational and legal realm of bureaucracy. In particular, anthropology has long interpreted conflicts between "formal rules" and informal practices as arising from the demands of conflicting normative orders. Such normative orientations have been considered to arise "outside" the office, emanating from social relations in which office holders are embedded. Obligations to acknowledge these relations give rise to deviations from official procedure. Inevitably, this leads to analyses that establish a dichotomy between society and the state, or between an intra-bureaucratic ethos of indifference and an extra-bureaucratic realm of moral normativity.

At the same time, much critique of bureaucracy has focused precisely on assumptions of its anethical nature. Many analyses encounter "Frankensteins: the rules guiding them can overwhelm the goals they are supposed to serve and the missions 'creep' continually outward. Bureaucrats [...] are at once inanimate – lazy automatons, blindly serving larger powers – and animate – nefarious, self-interested obstructionists" (Hoag 2011: 82). In his book on the Indian welfare bureaucracy (2012), Akhil Gupta, while acknowledging the ethical orientation of governmental programmes and individual civil servants, has advanced the thesis that the failures of the Indian state are found not in the divergence of state bureaucratic practices from proposed formal procedures, but within formal procedures that engender indifference towards the arbitrary outcomes they produce.[6] This echoes other critiques that consider bureaucratic practice to produce indifference (Herzfeld 1992), or point to the violence inherent in bureaucratic classification (Graeber 2015) or to the loss of moral responsibility (Bauman 1989). These analyses locate bureaucratic violence in excessive orientation towards bureaucratic procedures (rather than in the corruption of those procedures) and consider bureaucratic state apparatus a form of domination that rules according to instrumental-rational criteria dissociated from moral evaluation. For Bauman, the absence of moral evaluation in bureaucracies results from functional divisions of labour and the substitution of technical for moral responsibility. Functional division of tasks within and between bureaucratic authorities undermines the assumption of moral responsibility for the outcome of a collective activity, a phenomenon that Matthew Hull superbly demonstrated by tracing the erasure of individual authorship on administrative decisions (Hull 2003).[7] A system of fragmented responsibility allows the construction of holocaustic apparatus (Bauman 1989: 98), making possible the banalisation of evil.

---

6 Unlike others who point to the anethical nature of the administrative apparatus, Gupta claims that indifference to the arbitrariness of outcomes prevails despite the existence of ethical concerns on the part of individual civil servants and the overall goals of the administration.

7 Hull's examination is based on material from Pakistan's civil service. The erasure observed here, and the dissolution of attributable responsibility, has particular contextual reasons, as erasures of authorship are deeply entangled with civil servants' fear for their professional careers, a fear largely shaped by the politics of transfer in South Asia. This might take entirely different forms in other contexts, or be less pronounced in other administrations.

Could and should one read Hannah Arendt's thesis of the banality of evil as the possibility of a murderous ethic's normalisation and routinisation, rather than the anethical nature of bureaucracy? This reading might not accord with Arendt's notion of morality, since her normative concept of morals stressed the residual freedom of choice against obedience to the law. If, however, we ask whether the banality of evil did not necessitate first a *banalization* of evil,[8] we come to an empirical notion of ethics. Using an empirical notion of ethics enables us to differentiate between various co-existing ethics; it does not negate the possibility of moral resistance to public ethics, since public or bureaucratic ethics do not determine value orientations by obliterating all other moral or ethical norms. Rather, the ethics inherent in the substantive goals and purposes an "office" is tasked with impact the practices of office holders by shaping their "ideologically affected desires" (Gill 2009: 215).

Our approach to the ethics of office is akin to that of Didier Fassin in his recent discussion of "the heart of the state". He holds, and we agree, that state agents "work in reference to a certain professional ethos, to a training they have received, to an idea they have of their actions, and to a routine they develop. The principles of justice or of order, the values of the common good and public service, the attention to social or psychological realities [...] all products of their professional habitus, influence the way they will respond to state injunctions and behave towards their publics," (Fassin 2015b: 6-7). Fassin complicates analyses of the bureaucrat as "automaton" (Herzfeld 1992: 1) that often prevails in critiques of bureaucracies. Whereas he stresses the interrelation of professional ethics and affects (Fassin 2015a; Fassin 2015b: 10), we concentrate on the interrelation of the ethics of office and bureaucratic practice.

Employing this focus on the ethics of office also avoids the individualist bent implicit in many analyses of bureaucratic discretion. Anthropologies of bureaucrats often produce implicit assumptions about discretionary "freedom" simply by *not* focussing on precisely how discretion is *practised*, or rather, how it is shaped and structured in itself. Thus, ethnographic bottom-up perspectives on administration, policy or the state suffer from a lack of attention to the impact of formal rules and public ideologies – often due to the attempt to overcome reductionist top-down analyses that do not attend

---

8 Roland Eckert in a conversation in October 2018.

to variation in bureaucratic practice (see also Fassin 2015b: 5). In order to understand the particular sociality of bureaucratic discretion, and to understand "interpretation", "subsumption" and "application", I suggest that discretionary practices are informed by the ethos and the ethics that pertain to a specific bureaucracy at a given time and place, and that are trained and cultivated formally and informally in bureaucratic sociabilities, as Laura Affolter shows in her contribution to this volume (also see Affolter (2016) where she develops the term "institutional habitus" for this phenomenon). The "bureaucratic ethic" guides the application and interpretation of rules. Only with such an ethical basis, as Thomas Bierschenk and Jean Pierre Olivier de Sardan have also stressed (2014: 13), can discretion be exercised. "Worldview directs thought-work such as case interpretations. Therefore, organizational worldview fosters the subtle coherence of decisions over a wide variety of cases," Heyman says (1995: 265). Individual segments of bureaucracies relate interpreting their tasks to their specific role in achieving overall goals. Tasks precisely shape how rules are interpreted and implemented to serve these ends. They suggest which division of labour best aligns with an overall goal. They outline what responsibilities follow from ascribed competences, and which attribution of responsibility is "rational", questions that arise in relation to such quotidian matters as budget allocation, agency competition or assigning "cases" to specific bureaucratic agencies or "desks". What it is to do a job well, to be rule oriented (i.e. to interpret the rule), to be consistent, effective or efficient, these ambitions can only be achieved in the light of the broader ethical goals. Such matters of definition and interpretation are intrinsic to bureaucratic work; they establish how the commonweal is best served by a specific bureaucratic agency.

I want to hold on to the distinction described above that Weber made between ethos and ethics rather than merging the two terms, as might be possible through the notion of moral economy as used by Didier Fassin (2009). I find it useful to retain distinct notions of ethos and ethics as possible aspects of a moral economy of state bureaucracies at a specific time in a specific place, because they are not the same and they can be in tension with each other. Images of the state, as Klaus Schlichte and Joel Migdal noted (2005: 14), encompass both the substantive promise inherent in the purpose attributed to that state, which I call "bureaucratic ethics", and the procedures deemed "state-like" and proper that the state bureaucracy can use to fulfil that promise, which I call "bureaucratic ethos". Both are situated in the same historical moment and hold for the same social realm. They are inextricably linked, but can conflict, as I will explain below.

The moral community

Visions of what public goods the state is responsible for, and what procedures are appropriate for it to use to accomplish them, are subject to change. A state may be defined by goals of autonomy, modernization, equality or equity, competitive military or economic power or welfare; and its bureaucratic procedures judged by their efficacy, transparency, participatory nature or cost efficiency. Fundamentally, changes in ethos and ethics are expressed in how the moral community a bureaucracy is concerned with is differentiated and delineated, and how its relations to, and differential obligations towards its members and non-members are defined.

Contemporary visions of the commonweal of European nation states are entangled in contradictory imperatives. Deep tensions exist among the prerogative of the nation state to distinguish between insiders and outsiders, humanitarian appeals to broaden definitions of the greater good, and the global interdependencies that are a requisite for any common good. These simultaneous imperatives produce institutional contradictions, the resolution of which demands differential prioritisation.

In his contribution to this volume, David Loher shows how, in Swiss asylum procedures, the notion of voluntariness serves to align the imperative of the exclusionary nation state with humanitarian delegitimisation of state violence: the best and most ethical (but also the cheapest) way to exclude is when the excluded leave voluntarily. This ethical stance impacts the way officials who organise voluntary return migration understand their task, and how they go about achieving it. The notion of "voluntariness" discussed by Loher is central to current conceptualisations not only of human agency, but also of fairness, efficiency and efficacy.

Contradictions between imperatives of the nation state, the national economy and humanitarian ideals often come to the fore in competitions between bureaucratic agencies, particularly between those charged with bio-political duties and those with disciplinary and security tasks (see also Schiffauer in this volume; Fassin 2015b: 6).

Simon Affolter's chapter describes a smooth negotiation between the contradictory imperatives of upholding immigration law and labour law standards, on the one hand, and ensuring the ongoing provision of cheap migrant labour on which the Swiss commonweal depends, on the other. Cheaper labour is less regulated labour, particularly in an agricultural sector that has symbolic significance for Swiss national identity. Institutional inconsistencies arising between these principles are functional, Affolter shows us, in relation to the prioritisation of efficiency in Swiss agriculture, and as a means to preserve a symbol of national autarky. Enforcement of both labour law and immigration law is subordinate to the economic viability of Swiss agriculture (see Heyman 1995 for a discussion of the US situation). Thus, labour law and its enforcement has little relevance for serving the national conceptualisation of the commonweal. Individual officials situationally enact this hierarchisation of laws (and of administrative bureaus) by relying on the overall goal of serving a specific delineation of the Swiss common good.

Mediations between the diverse priorities of different state agencies are contingent upon many factors. The dominance of one discourse or one agency, which directs how best to secure the commonweal, might give way to other strategies and other agencies once economic or political expediencies change. Yet, prioritisations among contradictory imperatives of the commonweal remain embedded in historical legacies and influence contemporary functions.[9] The memory of "Weimar" as a frail state legitimises contemporary ethics of defensive democracy ("*wehrhafte Demokratie*"); this forms the horizon and legitimatory repertoire for many a bureaucratic norm in Germany, as Werner Schiffauer shows in his analysis of the symmetri-

---

9 Ethos and ethics change in shorter intervals in relation to mediatized events – but relations between media representations and public ethics appear to be somewhat dialogical, as media representations not only respond to but also shape public ethics. In what was called the "refugee crisis" we could observe daily shifts between a humanitarian perspective on the refugees from Syria struggling at eastern European borders, and a security perspective, ever differentiating the criteria for legitimate mobility, targeting both Syrian and less officially legitimate refugees (see also De Genova 2016). With such short term shifts, it is not always possible to tell whether a shift is relevant to ethical values, or whether it affects what, or how something can be legitimately addressed, i.e. a shift in rhetoric. Yet, shifts in rhetoric, taken "at their word", can trigger shifts in practice. Rhetoric sets standards and defines the norm or the normal, the way to view an issue.

cal construction of different "extremisms" in German security agencies. Chowra Makaremi employs the notion of memory to show how political considerations connected to both post-colonial memory and contemporary power relations shape the French asylum system. She highlights the colonially informed political stakes that underpin the selection of those who possess rights to national protection and others, as well as the ramifications of diplomatic affinities and tensions in the arena of asylum (e.g. France's position of withdrawal from regional issues in West Africa). Makaremi shows how the national host community is redefined, first literally through a process of filtering and excluding those who do not belong to it, and then figuratively, through affirmation of common rationalities and moral values, such as democratic assistance or protecting the welfare state against abuses and false refugees.

Knowing like a state

In many ways, ethos and ethics are intrinsic to administrative categorisation procedures. Bureaucracies process cases according to given (legal) categories of difference, so that differential access to rights defines multifaceted cases for singular purposes, and boundaries are set within the gradual, continuous character of difference (see Handelman 2004: 23). More importantly, bureaucracies create categorical differences according to their specific tasks and the perceived needs of the commonweal.

Thus, administrative categories are deeply ingrained in the way the state knows. Classificatory practices are based on knowledge, and at the same time shape what can be known. Knowledge is purposeful. Its selection is shaped by the problems that an agency is supposed to address. In his contribution, Werner Schiffauer examines the creation of task-specific categories and the kinds of functional blindness they produce. Schiffauer points out how a degree of "decisionism" inheres in the creation of any category.[10] At

---

10 Decisionism is the term employed by Carl Schmitt, who proposes that norms gain validity only through decisions (by the proper authority). These decisions are, at their core, unjustifiable as they can never be entirely explained by logical or ethical criteria (Schmitt 1922). For Schmitt, the validity of law was not inherent in its principles but made fact by the proper authority. Max Weber used the term slightly differently to seek a solution to the problems of rational legal rule. To him, legality alone could not set goals or make value

some point on the boundary between one category and the next, the differences between two cases in the same category might be greater than between two cases flanking both sides of the arbitrary divide. This ultimate arbitrariness defines administrative exercises in classification precisely because the boundary of a category cannot be logically or ethically explained in its entirety, but arbitrarily delimits gradual difference at a specific point. This decisionism is complemented by the "discretion" exercised in the application of categories of difference (see, e.g. Lipsky 1983), as to subsume a specific "case" under a categorical rubric necessitates interpretation by those who perform this application to such situations.

It might appear contradictory to claim that the categorical differentiations of (migration) bureaucracies are decisionist in nature, and hence not justifiable by logical or ethical norms, and yet that this decisionism is shaped by a bureaucratic ethic. In fact, this is precisely the point. Bureaucratic ethics "rationalise" the decisionism of bureaucratic categories because arbitrariness is anathema to rational legal rule. This is evident in Schiffauer's analysis of the categories of danger developed and continually differentiated by the German Office for the Protection of the Constitution as it struggles to keep up with the intellectual dynamics of Islamic communities. What is also evident is the futility of these efforts. Bureaucrats are usually aware of the poor fit of these categories with actual "cases" they work on. In response to tensions between category and case phenomena, new categories are created with even finer differentiations. But they remain anachronistic snapshots of an intrinsically dynamic field. Nonetheless, even failed categories are often highly productive of social order. As Schiffauer shows, they gain a truth-value beyond their specific purposes.

Everyday states of exception, or: Does it really matter what they think they do?

While the norms of ethos and ethics are both intrinsic aspects of bureaucratic practice, ethos and ethics are not the same. They can conflict, especially when shifts in fashion affect proper procedure (such as the introduc-

---

decisions; only a leader's decision(-ism) could save modern society from the iron cage of rationalisation (Weber 1919).

tion of public management techniques; see Bear and Mathur 2015) or when changes occur in public ethics.

This tension comes to the fore in the reasoning of the return migration bureaucrats to whom David Loher spoke. Their defence of rule-orientation rests on the principle of equal treatment, without implying approval of the substantive ethics behind the rules they enforce. They prioritise "rule-following – and therefore procedural or formal justice – over substantive justice" Loher continues: "Identification of the principle of rule-orientation with fairness indicates that there is more at stake than concern about pure procedure" (Loher, this volume). He holds that, in this case, ethos is ethics.

However, when the norms of ethos are perceived as hindering service to the commonweal, ethics sometimes trumps ethos. Just as substantive goals and values can be overridden by procedural concerns – as in "automaton" accounts of bureaucracy – so can procedural ethoses be overridden by adherence to substantive ethics. As Fassin also observes: "whether through over zealousness or conviction the agents often extend the realm of policies well beyond what is requested" (2015b: 5). Bureaucrats might believe in their office. They might believe in ethos and ethics alike, or they might prioritise ethics, i.e. specific orientations towards the commonweal, over procedural concerns. Bureaucratic ethics import the Dirty Harry problem (Klockars 1980) into governmental apparatus.[11] To put it another way, ethics in tension with ethos calls forth a myriad of situational states of exception.

Everyday states of exception, when law is suspended in order to safeguard the legal order (Schmitt 1922) are particularly evident in Nicholas De

---

11 It is important to point out the possibility of prioritisation to complement the image of "the automaton", and bring to light bureaucrats' commitment to their offices, the "volitional allegiance" that Gill spoke about (2009: 215). Furthermore, dedication in pursuit of the larger goals an office is tasked with to the detriment of procedural rules can be no less problematic than mere rule orientation. This is why Du Gay (2000) praises the democratic potentials of bureaucratic rule orientation. Detecting everyday states of exception in the Dirty Harries of bureaucratic practice, tension between ethos and ethics in bureaucracies might come down to an image of the heroic civil servant acting solely in an attempt to serve the goals he or she is tasked with. This critical point was made by Klaus Schlichte in discussion of a draft version of this article. I consider ethical orientations towards an office to be far more quotidian than any notion of heroism would imply. Such an ethical orientation is not "exceptional", but rather, a matter of work ethics, and of labour explored as practice, which encompasses habits, routines, skills, value orientations, decision making, etc.

Genova's examination of "detainability". De Genova shows how "the lowest level enforcers of the law must constantly exercise their own discretion and routinely decide on a case-by-case basis on the 'state of exception' between the abstraction of the law and the fact of violence that enforces it, in the putative interest of 'order' or 'security'" (this volume). Everyday states of exception are equally present in Affolter's Swiss agricultural sector, where labour officers establish a situational hierarchy of legal norms (only some of which are enforced) related to their orientation towards serving the commonweal of Switzerland. The systematic and systemically related violation of labour and immigration law is a functional prerequisite of serving the commonweal as currently defined.

Evident in both examples is how everyday states of exception are governed by many rules. This echoes what Nasser Hussain has called "hyper-legality" (2007). Hussain responded to the easy Agambian assumption of "law-less" or extra-legal spaces of exception, and showed how the rule of law actually made possible and regulated such exceptions. This insight is important for us insofar as it demands a process-based approach to the exploration of ethos and ethics, one that can bring to light how, in the continuously alternating prioritisation of one over the other, institutional change is produced. In quotidian states of exception, such as the cases discussed above, changes in the image of the state, in its ethics and its proper procedures, also encompass a complicated relation between legality and legitimacy. Changes in legitimacy occur at different rhythms than changes in legality. More importantly, legal procedures considered inappropriate for reaching certain state goals can lose legitimacy, whereas illegal procedures and practices can become legitimate when perceived as effective in fulfilling state promises. Small discrepancies might lead to incremental shifts in the interpretation of legal rules by state officers; stark discrepancies might lead to an open departure from legal rule and legitimate practice (as perceived by office holders).

Prioritisation of substantive goals over procedural norms is often followed by procedural adjustments. Legal reform realigns the legality and legitimacy of administrative practice. The discretionary margin is widened and executive powers are enhanced (see e.g. Eckert 2012). Central to realignments of legitimacy and legality are notions of threat and crisis (see also Fassin 2015b: 2) that justify drawing lines between those considered to belong, and enjoy specific protections, and those outside the moral community that a bureaucratic ethic is concerned with. This is why paying attention to the dynamic tension between bureaucratic ethos and ethics is important, and why acknowledging their distinction has heuristic value.

Conclusion

While acknowledging the myriad constraints, diverse goals and contradictory logics bureaucrats are entangled in, as well as the possible influence of personal and public morals (Fassin 2015), the point here is to refocus attention on the ethics of office. Dynamics born of relations between ethos and ethics, and their impact on bureaucratic practice, have not been adequately addressed in recent literature on the anthropology of bureaucracy or policy. Too focussed on either rule-orientation or discretionary freedom, many approaches have overlooked the way interpretations of the commonweal shape bureaucratic practice. We stress that such interpretations cannot be considered extra-bureaucratic ethical concerns, but are intrinsic to the profession (see also Bierschenk and Olivier de Sardan 2014: 12-13; Lentz 2014). Certainly, situations exist where orientation towards the public good is not of great importance in the conduct of public servants; in such situations many factors possibly contribute to a minimal identification with the job (see, e.g. Bierschenk 2014. 222). In many other situations, however, viewing oneself as a public servant who serves a public good is fundamental to the way people conduct their work. This holds true, I would claim, in such diverse situations as in the Indian police service (Eckert 2005), among Ghanaian public servants (Lentz 2015) or in the situations explored in the contributions to this volume. However, where such orientations hold sway and how they develop or diminish is an empirical question. Differences might arise not only in accord with the states in question and the historical moments of analysis, but also in different areas of state administration. Ethos and ethics are highly contextual, and so is their relevance for bureaucratic practice.

At the same time, attention to the ethos and ethics of office is as essential to understanding bureaucratic practice as attention to extra-bureaucratic expediencies. The notion of the office, of professionalism in civil service, even of ubiquitous laments about failure, corruption or inadequacy confirm the relevance of the ethics of office to understanding the work of bureaucracies. They define the ways a commonweal is best served and delineate its moral community. Furthermore, differentiating between the ethos and ethics of bureaucracies and investigating the dynamics that arise from their relations can provide insights into institutional and legal change. Bureaucrats' quotidian struggles to align ethos and ethics, or to justify their divergence, bring about incremental changes that sometimes need normative acknowledgement to effect legal reform.

Bibliography

Affolter, Laura. 2016. *Taking Decisions in a Swiss Asylum Administration. 'Institutonal Habitus' and Patterns of Practice.* Manuscript, on file with the author.

Arendt, Hannah. 1968. *The Origins of Totalitarianism*. New York: Harcourt.

Bauman, Zygmunt. 1989. *Modernity and the Holocaust*. Ithaca: Cornell University Press.

Bear, Laura, and Nayanika Mathur. 2015. Introduction. Remaking the Public Good – A New Anthropology of Bureaucracy. *The Cambridge Journal of Anthropology*, 33(1): 18–34.

Bierschenk, Thomas. 2014. Sedimentation, Fragmentation and Normative Double-Binds in (West) African Public Service. In Thomas Bierschenk and Jean-Pierre Olivier de Sardan, eds, *States at Work. Dynamics of African Bureaucracies*. Leiden: Brill: 221–247.

Bierschenk, Thomas, and Jean-Pierre Olivier de Sardan. 2014. Studying the Dynamics of African Bureaucracies. An Introduction to States at Work. In Thomas Bierschenk and Jean-Pierre Olivier de Sardan, eds, *States at Work. Dynamics of African Bureaucracies*. Leiden: Brill: 3–34.

Cancik, Pascale. 2004. "Selbst ist das Volk" - Der Ruf nach "Volkstümlichkeit der Verwaltung" in der ersten Hälfte des 19. Jahrhunderts. *Der Staat*, 43: 298–327.

De Genova, Nicholas. 2016. The 'Crisis' of the European Border Regime. Towards a Marxist Theory of Borders. *International Socialism. A Quarterly Review of Socialist Theory*, [online] 150, available at: http.//isj.org.uk/the-crisis-of-the-european-border-regime-towards-a-marxist-theory-of-borders/ [accessed 6 Jan 2017].

Du Gay, Paul. 2000. *In Praise of Bureaucracy; Weber, Organisation, Ethics*. London: Sage.

Eckert, Julia. 2005. The Trimurti of the State. *Sociologus*, II: 181–217.

Eckert, Julia. 2012. Theories of Militancy in Practice. Explanations of Muslim Terrorism in India. *The Social Science History Journal*, 36(3): 47–72.
Fassin, Didier. 2009. Les économies morales revisitées. *Annales Histoire, Sciences sociales*, 6: 1237–1266.
Fassin, Didier. 2012. Toward a Critical Moral Anthropology.. In Didier Fassin, ed., *A Companion to Moral Anthropology*. Oxford: Wiley: 1–17.
Fassin, Didier. 2015a. Can States Be Moral? In Didier Fassin, ed., *The Heart of the State*, London: Pluto, ix–xi.
Fassin, Didier. 2015b. Introduction. Governing Precarity. In Didier Fassin, ed., *The Heart of the State*. London: Pluto: 1–14.
Gill, Nick. 2009. Presentational State Power. Temporal and Spatial Influence Over Asylum Sector Decisionmakers. *Transactions*, 34: 215–233.
Graeber, David. 2015. *The Utopia of Rules; on Technology, Stupidity, and the Secret Joys of Bureaucracy*. New York: Melville House.
Gupta, Akhil. 2012. *Red Tape. Bureaucracy, Structural Violence, and Poverty in India*. Durham: Duke University Press.
Handelman, Don. 1981. Introduction. The Idea of Bureaucratic Organization. *Social Analysis*, 9: 5–23.
Handelman, Don. 2004. *Nationalism and the Israeli State*. Oxford: Berg.
Herzfeld, Michael. 1992. *The Social Production of Indifference. Exploring the Symbolic Roots of Western Bureaucracy*. New York: Berg.
Hoag, Colin. 2011. Assembling Partial Perspectives. Thoughts on the Anthropology of Bureaucracy. *PoLAR, Political and Legal Anthropology Review*, 34(1): 81–94.
Heyman, Josiah. 1995. Putting Power in the Anthropology of Bureaucracy. The Immigration and Naturalization Service at the Mexico-United States Border. *Current Anthropology*, 36(2): 261–287.
Hull, Matthew S. 2003. *Government of Paper. The Materiality of Bureaucracy in Urban Pakistan*. Berkeley: University of California Press.
Hussain, Nasser. 2007. Beyond Norm and Exception: Guantánamo. *Critical Inquiry*, 33(4): 734–753.
Klockars, Carl. 1980. The Dirty Harry Problem. *Annals of the American Academy of Political and Social Science*, 452: 33–47.
Lentz, Carola. 2014. "I Take an Oath to the State, Not the Government". Career Trajectories and Professional Ethics of Ghanaian Public Servants. In Thomas Bierschenk and Jean-Pierre Olivier de Sardan, eds, *States at Work. Dynamics of African Bureaucracies*. Leiden: Brill: 175–204.

Lipsky, Michael. 1983. *Street Level Bureaucrats*. New York: Russel Sage Foundation.

Olivier de Sardan, Jean-Pierre. 2009. Practical Norms. Informal Regulation Within Public Bureaucracies (in Africa and Beyond). In Tom De Herdt and Jean-Pierre Olivier de Sardan, eds, *Real Governance and Practical Norms in Sub-Saharan Africa. The Game of the Rules*. London: Routledge: 19–62.

Osborne, Thomas. 1994. Bureaucracy As a Vocation. Governmentality and Administration in Nineteenth-Century Britain. *Journal of Historical Sociology*, 7(3): 289–313.

Schlichte, Klaus and Joel Migdal. 2005. Rethinking the State. In Klaus Schlichte, ed., *The Dynamics of States*. Aldershot: Ashgate: 1–40.

Schmitt, Carl. 1922. *Politische Theologie. Vier Kapitel zur Lehre von der Souveränität*. München und Leipzig: Duncker & Humblot.

Swedberg, Richard. 2005. *The Max Weber Dictionary; Key Words and Central Concepts*. Stanford: Stanford University Press.

Weber, Max 1919. *Politik als Beruf*. München und Leipzig: Duncker und Humblot.

Wedel, Janine R., Cris Shore, Gregory Feldman and Stacy Lathrop. 2005. Toward an Anthropology of Public Policy. *Annals of the American Academy of Political and Social Science*, 600: 30–51.

Keeping Numbers Low in the Name of Fairness
Ethos and Ethics in a Swiss Asylum Administration

Laura Affolter

Introduction

"I am interested in foreigners, other cultures. The basic idea is to help these people, even if we do – of course – reject many of them", Gabriel, a caseworker in the Swiss Secretariat for Migration (SEM), once said to me (Gabriel, caseworker, interview transcript).[1] The SEM is where first-instance asylum decisions are made in Switzerland. Officials working there – officials like Gabriel – make decisions about whether asylum seekers fulfil the requirements for refugee status, and whether they believe the applicants' statements are credible.[2] Applicants must fulfil both preconditions before receiving asylum. Although Gabriel works in the SEM "to help people", for him it is okay that most applicants get rejected. This has to do with his understanding of *fairness*, a core issue in professional decision-making. Thus, later in the conversation quoted above, he went on to say that it was the decision-makers' duty to meticulously examine the credibility of each case, because otherwise "everybody could just receive asylum and that would be unfair to those who

---

1 All the names in this chapter are pseudonyms.
2 I use the terms "asylum seekers", "applicants" and "claimants" because they are the emic terms SEM officials employ and it is their perspectives that I critically engage with in this paper. However, I am aware that labels carry meanings and, by using them, there is the danger of reproducing them. Labels do not "exist in a vacuum" but are "the tangible representation of policies and programs", Zetter argues (2007: 180). Hence, only through entering the asylum system do "people on the move" become "asylum seekers" (ibid.: 175). In fact, the term "asylum seeker" fits with the shift that Fassin (2016) describes from asylum as a right to asylum as a favour (see also Jubany 2011: 85).

really deserve asylum, who really need protection" (ibid.).³ Gabriel's statement exemplifies a common view within the SEM that, in order for decision-making to be fair, granting asylum and temporary protection must be reserved exclusively for those "truly deserving of it". Fairness is, therefore, based on exclusion.

The exclusionary workings (in particular, the outcomes) of asylum decision-making have been widely criticised (see, for instance, Harvey 1997; Jubany 2017; Marfleet 2006; Scheffer 2001; Souter 2011; Zimmermann 2011). By tracing historical changes in asylum and refugee policy, several studies have shown how asylum policies and asylum law started to become more restrictive in the early 1980s as applicants increasingly fell outside the East/West, communist/non-communist divide, and after the 1970s recession increased unemployment, which led to restrictions on labour immigration (see, for instance, Däpp 1984; Fassin 2013: 8ff; Fassin & Kobelinsky 2012: 448ff; Piguet 2006). Furthermore, they describe how, in the 1980s, a discourse about "false" or "bogus" refugees trying to abuse the system emerged as the number of asylum applications increased (Däpp 1984: 216ff; see also Fassin 2007). In Switzerland, this "fight against abuse" has been the driving force behind and the means of legitimating many of the restrictions made in Swiss asylum law in the past thirty-seven years (see Miaz 2017: 83ff). However, these historical accounts do not tell us much about how such policies or policy changes are translated into practice and shaped and mediated in this process (see, for instance, Lipsky 2010; Shore and Wright 1997, 2011; Wedel et al. 2005). Furthermore, while they show how the eligibility criteria for refugee status or for receiving temporary protection have gradually become more restrictive, they offer little explanation as to why most asylum applications are rejected on the basis of so-called "non-credibility".⁴

---

3 I use the term "decision-makers" for the SEM officials who conduct asylum interviews and write decisions. Final decisions bear their signatures and also that of their direct superiors. As I will show in this contribution, decision-makers' decisions can by changed by their superiors. Hence, the superiors also become decision-makers in a way. For a critical reflection on the term "decision-maker", see Lavanchy and Garros (forthcoming). Here, I use the terms "decision-maker", "caseworker" and "(SEM) official" synonymously, separating them from the heads of the asylum units, whom I call "superiors".

4 Unfortunately, negative asylum decisions are registered with the same code regardless of whether they are made on the basis of "non-credibility" (article 7 of the Swiss Asylum Act, AsylA), of non-eligibility for refugee status (article 3 AsylA) or a combination of both. It is

Kelly, who in *Sympathy and Suspicion: Torture, Asylum, and Humanity* "explore[s] the epistemological conditions under which it is possible to doubt or deny the claim of others" (2012: 755), offers one explanation. He argues that "the very process of imagined identification found in compassion can lie behind suspicion" (ibid.: 753). Several other authors have argued that elements of "non-credibility" – and through them "lies" and individuals labelled as "liars" – are actively created by means of decision-making processes, particularly through the questioning techniques used in asylum interviews (see Crawley 1999: 52ff; Sbriccoli and Jacoviello 2011: 184ff; Scheffer 2001, 2003; Trueman 2009: 296ff). This argument challenges the common explanation put forward by asylum administrations, politicians and much of the mainstream media that the majority of claims are rejected because the majority of asylum seekers lie. Building on both these approaches, I examine what makes it *normal* and *desirable* for "otherwise compassionate and rational people" (Kelly 2012: 755) to doubt and deny the claims of others. In other words, how does it become routine for decision-makers to adopt questioning strategies that actively generate indicators of "non-credibility"?

I approach this question by empirically exploring what SEM decision-makers think they should be doing. Following Eckert's argument in the introduction of this volume, I claim that what "bureaucrats" do is shaped by what they think they should do.[5] What they think they should do, in turn, is shaped by both the ethics and ethos of the office. Eckert (this volume) defines bureaucratic ethics as the "values and norms associated with the substantive goals of a bureaucratic apparatus geared towards ideas of a good society,

---

therefore not possible to quantitatively analyse what reasons were cited for negative decisions. However, the SEM online manual on asylum and return (*Asyl und Rückkehr*) states that the majority of rejections are attributable to the lack of credibility of asylum seekers' claims (https://www.sem.admin.ch/dam/data/sem/asyl/verfahren/hb/c/hb-c5-d.pdf [accessed 19 September 2018]. In addition, all of my interaction partners (both SEM decision-makers and legal advisors) were of the impression that most negative decisions are based on non-credibility. In Affolter (2018) I discuss different reasons why it is an institutional preference to argue negative decisions on the basis of "non-credibility", rather than on "non-eligibility for refugee status".

5 The terms "bureaucracy" and "bureaucrats" carry negative connotations. They are often associated with "red tape" and "officialism" and used as criticism (Eckert, this volume; Poertner 2017: 12). Here, I mostly use the terms "administration" and "office". However, when referring to literature that uses the terms "bureaucracy" and "bureaucrats", I employ the same terminology.

good life, welfare, or justice". Thus, the term "bureaucratic ethics" stands for the specific purposes of a bureaucracy; the goals its employees are tasked with, both explicitly and implicitly. Bureaucratic ethos, on the other hand, describes the assemblage of procedural behaviours deemed proper for fulfilling these purposes (ibid.). Taking up Eckert's argument that bureaucracies are not anethical, as Bauman (2000), Graeber (2015) and Herzfeld (1992) have claimed, but rather that ethics are "intrinsic to bureaucratic work", I show how the ethics of office shape its procedural values: the ethos of the office. That is, decision-makers' understanding of *what* their role is shapes their understanding of *how* to carry it out professionally. Since what "bureaucrats" think they should do informs their everyday practices, and their everyday practices shape and mediate the policies and laws they are charged with implementing (see, for instance, Silbey 2005: 324; Wedel et al. 2005: 34), we need to explore the ethics and ethos of the office in order to understand how asylum law and policies work. Furthermore, as Fassin (2015:4) has stated, paying attention to state officials – their "actions, routines, values and feelings" – is crucial to understanding how the state works.

This chapter consists of four main parts. Part one describes a field episode in which two SEM officials – a superior and his employee – discuss the rightfulness of a decision. From that point of departure I extract, in part two, what the officials as decision-makers consider their duties to be. Their conceptualisations form the basis for deriving the ethics of the office. In part three I discuss a variety of norms associated with the notion of being professional in the SEM. Particularly through the norm of fairness, we see how procedural ethos is shaped by bureaucratic ethics. Part four shows how the ethics and ethos of the office make one particular decision-making practice, which I call "digging deep", the normal and desirable thing for decision-makers to do. "Digging deep", in turn, leads to reaffirmation of the office's norms and values.

This paper is based on ethnographic material from fieldwork for my PhD, which was conducted in the SEM during various stays between 2014 and 2015. I shadowed decision-makers from various organisational units in their work, observing them as they wrote decisions, prepared and conducted asylum interviews, chatted to colleagues in hallways and during coffee breaks, helped each other with difficult "cases", performed administrative tasks and participated in team meetings.⁶ Furthermore, I took part in a three-week training session for new employees, conducted semi-structured interviews with decision-makers and superiors from nine different units in the SEM and analysed case files.

Negotiating "the right" decision: a field anecdote

A decision-maker, Rebecca, and her superior, Alfredo, are discussing a decision she has made. As Rebecca's superior, it is Alfredo's duty to check and countersign her decisions before they are sent to the applicants. In this case, he does not agree with Rebecca's decision to grant temporary protection to a family from Iraq. I quote this excerpt from my field notes in detail because it brings to light several aspects of what Alberto and Rebecca believe professional decision-making involves.

I am sitting in Alberto's office, watching him go through his employees' decisions and case files. The documents he appraises, decisions that need his signature before they can go out, were left by his employees on a table outside his office. The first decision he picks up is a negative one for a family from Iraq. Yet, the decision-maker, Rebecca, has granted the family temporary protection. For my benefit, Alberto comments on the decision as he reads through it. I learn that the family came to Switzerland a couple of years ago because the husband started work with a human rights organisation. When the husband's contract ended, the family stayed on and filed for asylum.

Alberto tells me that he agrees with the negative decision. He says the family's problems do not qualify them as refugees. Then, looking at the internal application for temporary protection Rebecca has submitted, he says: "Ok, the kids are still quite young and they've been here for quite a while, so they haven't lived in their country of origin for a long time. But someone else might still have decided differently". He feels that it is a very "generous" decision. "I mean", he goes on, "they're an upper-class family. It wouldn't be a problem for them to be socially reintegrated. [...] They're a family, they're together, they can travel. They could go anywhere they want". Alberto is not quite sure what to do about the case, but he feels he cannot just let it pass

---

6 "Cases" is an emic term. Of course, what SEM decision-makers really deal with are not cases but people whose lives are greatly affected by their practices and decisions.

like that. In the end, he decides to put it aside for two hours and then return to it. Quickly, he goes through the other decisions from the pile on his desk, reading through them, flicking through the case files and then countersigning them. Once he has finished with the other decisions, he turns back to the case of the Iraqi family even though the two hours have not yet passed.

Seemingly out of the blue, and slightly defensively, he says to me: "The question of nation states and whether one thinks nation states are good or not, has nothing to do with what we do here. It cannot be solved by what we do. I'm all for granting protection", he continues, "but we don't have to hand it to them on a plate" (*aber man muss es den Leuten nicht nachschiessen*). He explains to me that seeing so many cases over the past several years has made him stricter and less naïve. What is important to him is that whatever leaves his desk is fair. This, he explains, also means protecting the asylum system from abuse. Saying that, he grabs the Iraqi family's case file and tells me he will take the decision back to the caseworker, Rebecca, to discuss it with her. He says that she will either have to add more reasons for granting the family temporary protection or reconsider her decision. Alberto asks if I would like to join him. Slightly hesitant, but also curious, I follow him to Rebecca's office.

Alberto explains to Rebecca that he thinks this is a very opportunistic, upper class family that does not need temporary protection. Rebecca says that she can see his point, but she worries that because the children are still quite young, their decision denying the family temporary protection might be quashed if case is taken on appeal to the Federal Administrative Court (FAC). "Also", she argues, "the wife has health problems". But Alberto does not think her problems are severe enough. He also does not think that the young children's not having lived in their country of origin would pose a problem in the event of an appeal, and he feels that the risk is worth taking. Together they discuss other possible "obstacles to removal", but Rebecca had already ruled them all out after consulting the *Federführung*.[7]

---

7 *Federführungen* are SEM officials who hold lead positions for particular "countr[ies] of origin". They are responsible for (co-)determining and monitoring the institution's decision-making practices in dealing with cases from these countries.

The discussion ends with the following dialogue:

Alberto: "I think the decision is too generous".
Rebecca: "That's my problem. I'm too nice."
Alberto: "I'm also nice."
Rebecca: "Yes, of course".

Alberto and Rebecca agree that she will work on the case again and rethink her original decision. Before leaving to go back to his office Alberto asks Rebecca whether she "can live with" this new decision. Rebecca assures Alberto that she can, and that she will still be able to sleep at night. She promises that it will not take her long to change the decision.

As Alberto and I set off towards his office again, Rebecca holds me back, causing Alberto to come back too. She explains to me that this is just a normal part of the job. Sometimes, though not often, decisions are given back and one has to work on them again. She says that in this case she was probably influenced by the fact that she had interviewed the family herself and that they had come across as being very pleasant. Alberto says that he finds this understandable and that this is something that has really changed for him since he was put in charge of the subdivision and stopped doing asylum interviews himself. "I have become stricter, because I see so many cases", he explains, "but I can also see things more clearly now, from a certain distance, more objectively".

This ethnographic vignette could be analytically explored in several different directions. Here, I limit myself to mapping out both Alberto's and Rebecca's understandings of professional decision-making. Professional norms that directly contribute to the exclusionary understanding of fairness posited at the beginning of this paper will be analysed in more detail later.

Rebecca and Alberto mention several different aspects of what they believe professional decision-making involves. From Alberto we learn that professional decision-making is fair, objective and apolitical. The latter characteristic he expresses by saying that one's personal opinion of nation states (and of the restrictions on freedom of movement and residence associated with them) has nothing to do with their job. He also has clear ideas of what constitutes fair and objective decision-making. For Alberto, fair decision-making relates to strictly following the law, and objective decision-making to making decisions "from a distance" and not becoming too personally involved in the case. From Rebecca, we learn that being a good and professional decision-maker means working fast, not becoming too personally involved in one's cases, and making decisions that one can personally endorse. We further infer from this anecdote that being naïve, "too generous" and "too nice" are considered to be features of unprofessional decision-making. Protection should be granted, but not too easily. In Alberto's words: "It shouldn't be handed to asylum seekers on a plate."

In order to understand why all of this has come to define professionalism for Rebecca and Alberto, I turn to the ethics of the office to demonstrate how it can be derived from what caseworkers understand their duties as decision-makers and state officials to be.

Ethics of the office: decision-makers as protectors of the system

In this field anecdote, Rebecca seems to be primarily occupied with what the FAC might think about her decision in case it is appealed. She worries that if she does not grant the family temporary protection, her decision might get quashed by the court for two reasons: first, because the children have never lived in what is referred to as their "country of origin" and it could be seen as unreasonable (or illegitimate) to send them "back", and second, because the mother has health problems.[8] Hence, Rebecca regards one of her main duties to be the making of "correct decisions", i.e., decisions that will not be quashed by the FAC.[9]

Generally, this is also considered important by her superiors. However, in this particular case, Alberto finds issuing a removal order for the family a risk worth taking because he deems two other duties to be of greater importance than trying to avoid a quashed decision. These duties are, on the one hand, to make sure that only those "really deserving of protection" receive

---

8 Rebecca fears that by issuing a removal order she might be defying article 3 of the UN Convention on the Rights of the Child.

9 Not having one's decisions quashed is important for two reasons. First, SEM units "keep records of how many of their employees' decisions are quashed" (Affolter et al. 2019: 270). Too many quashings is regarded as bad decision-making. Second, quashings stand in the way of fast and efficient decision-making (another important professional norm), since decision-makers often have to work on those cases again.

protection and, on the other hand, to protect the system from being abused by "undeserving" applicants. For Alberto, the Iraqi family does not deserve protection because, as an "upper class family", they are not sufficiently vulnerable. They do not fit the image of victims in need of help.[10] "They could go anywhere they want", he claims. This dual duty of protecting people – but only deserving people – and filtering out the undeserving in order to protect "the system" becomes apparent in the wording the SEM uses to describe the "[b]asic principles of asylum legislation" on its website:

> It is the duty of asylum proceedings to identify those asylum seekers among the new arrivals who are entitled to protection under the terms [of the Geneva Convention]. Many asylum seekers cannot be classified as refugees or persons displaced by war. On the basis of their situation, they clearly belong to the group of migrants. They are in search of a better place to live in Switzerland. Knowing that they would hardly obtain an entry or work permit, they cross the border illegally. Many of them invent a dramatic story of persecution for the hearing by the authorities. With such tactics they hope to be granted refugee status. From the viewpoint of the person concerned, this behaviour is understandable, from the perspective of asylum legislation it constitutes abuse of asylum proceedings. The authorities must reject such applications without delay and execute removal systematically, making asylum proceedings unattractive for foreigners seeking employment.[11]

The quote illustrates a common assumption within the SEM that many (or even most) asylum seekers will lie. While deemed understandable ("anyone in that situation would do it", I was often told), it is, nevertheless, the decision-makers' duty to separate the "real" from the "false" refugees, the ones "telling the truth" from the ones "who are lying" (see also Fassin & Kobelinsky 2012: 446; Kobelinsky 2015: 67). This is regarded as important because the asylum system is only seen to work if those "not deserving of protection"

---

10 Several authors have shown that asylum (and immigration) politics, law and decision-making produce a very particular "'figure' (Fassin 2007: 512) of the deserving aid recipient, framing him or her as a victim in need of protection" (Cabot 2013: 453; see, for instance, Ticktin 2006; Zetter 2007).

11 https://perma.cc/ZG4B-NN6U [accessed 22 August 2019].

are denied asylum. This quote from Miaz's fieldwork shows this distinction nicely:

> I think that saying "no" to someone who's not a refugee in the sense of the UNHCR and of the Refugee Convention contributes to the protection of the asylum institution. One has to say "no" to those who are not refugees in order to be able to say "yes" to those who are (Affolter et al. 2019: 273).

Similarly, Fassin and Kobelinsky have argued that "[t]he less frequently [asylum] is granted, the more precious refugee status becomes" (2012: 464). Thus, in order to maintain the value of asylum, many applications need to be rejected (ibid.: 465). Furthermore, the quote from the SEM website states that it is decision-makers' duty to make "asylum proceedings unattractive for foreigners seeking employment". I would argue that it is as much about making applying for asylum in Switzerland generally unattractive, or, at least not "as attractive" in comparison with other European countries. On the first day of training, new decision makers are told: "You are going to hear this often from now on: We are always afraid of the 'pull-effect'" (field notes). The assumption is that if Switzerland is "too generous in the granting of asylum (and humanitarian protection) compared to other countries", many more people will come (Poertner 2017: 17). Hence, although not officially stated, it follows that the office aims to keep both the number of new applications, and the number of successful applications low. That keeping numbers low is a decision-maker's duty was a message repeatedly conveyed in induction training. It may not have been explicitly taught, but it was consistently implied, as the following examples show.

In one of the training courses I attended, the instructor presented us with a graph comparing the number of new asylum applications in Europe and in Switzerland between 1998 and 2014. The graph showed that, in 2014, the percentage of asylum applicants in Switzerland was at its lowest point since 1998, dropping from 8.2% in 2012 to 3.8% in 2014. Drawing attention to this, the instructor commented: "Switzerland must have done something right, since the percentage of applications has gone down like this" (field notes). The message was quite clear. If "Switzerland" – partially through its frontline decision-makers – did its job well, this reduced the number of applications (especially in comparison with other European countries).

The second example comes from a course on how to deal with applications for family reunification. The instructor told the new decision-makers that the institutional practice for dealing with Eritrean applications was to request DNA proof that the applicants were indeed related to the people they intended to bring to Switzerland. The instructor said: "If they do not hand in DNA proof, the case is ready to be decided, namely negatively. I have seen that people have still been granted entry in such cases. Please don't do that. That's the worst signal we could be sending out" (field notes). With this statement, the instructor urged trainees to make sure their decision-making did not send out the wrong message to avoid creating a "pull-effect". The wrong message is that Switzerland is a country where family reunification is as easy as circumventing the regulations.

The two substantial goals the office is geared towards can be deduced from the examples above. As a Federal institution, the SEM – and, therefore, its staff – are requested to represent "national interests". On the one hand, this means fulfilling Switzerland's duties under international law (particularly the Geneva Convention and the UN Convention on the Rights of the Child) and maintaining its self-ascribed image as a humanitarian country. Upholding the noble value of asylum succeeds by excluding those "undeserving" of it. The scarcer asylum protection becomes, the more precious its value. On the other hand, it also means securing Switzerland's "borders" by restricting non-citizens' access to rights and goods, and by making sure that there are not too many "foreigners" residing in Switzerland. My analysis subsumes both sets of practices within the phrase "protecting the system", which, via two ostensibly opposed logics, comes to mean keeping numbers of asylum applicants low. This is at least partly achieved by keeping acceptance rates low. Decision-makers become "guardians of a restricted good": the right to reside in Switzerland (Heyman 2009: 381; see also Lipsky 2010: 4). My point here is not to say that all decision-makers consciously strive towards keeping numbers low. Many explicitly do not. However, I argue that the ethical goals of the office shape decision-makers' understanding of what it means to do their job well.

This is illustrated by the widespread language usage I encountered amongst decision-makers in the SEM. The verb most commonly used in granting asylum is "have to", whereas for rejecting asylum claims it is "can". Decision-makers typically say things like: "In that case I will *have to* grant asylum". Or: "If I had better arguments, I *could* reject this claim, but I *can't* like this". This language usage is not something decision-makers seem to be aware of, but it is also common amongst caseworkers prone to criticising colleagues for being "too strict" or "cynics" who want to reject as many asylum claims as possible (see Affolter et al. 2019; Miaz 2017: 371ff). This particular language usage shows how the role of protector of the system is adopted and internalised by decision-makers. It becomes part of their institutional habitus, which, building on Bourdieu, I define as the schemes of thinking, acting, feeling and desiring that arise from an official's position in the SEM (Bourdieu 1976; see Terdiman 1987: 811).[12] Protecting the system becomes the self-evident priority for decision-makers, as can be seen in the following example. While discussing a text in which I had written that the (implicit) goal of decision-making practices was to protect the system, a caseworker said to me: "Ok, yes, you could put it like this, but you could also phrase it as loyalty. That would be a bit more positive" (field notes). Although intended as critique, this remark actually reinforces my analytical point. For the SEM official, loyalty refers to being loyal towards a particular actor: the state. Whereas we could picture other loyalties, towards asylum seekers, for example, it is self-evident to the official that being loyal means putting what he sees as the state's interests first. This understanding of loyalty shapes the norms and values that define what it means to be professional in the SEM.

The good decision-maker: professional ethos

This section explores the professional norms and values that lie at the heart of everyday decision-making. In the SEM, the idea of fairness builds on many other professional values: apolitical-ness, objectivity, (emotional) detachment, professional suspicion (or non-naïvety) and strict rule-following. Subsequent sections deal with individual norms in more detail, showing how they both reinforce and conflict with each other.

---

12 I develop the concept of the "institutional habitus" in more detail in my thesis (see Affolter 2017a: 10ff).

The fair decision-maker

Alberto tells me that for him it is very important that all the asylum decisions leaving his section are fair. That is why he does not want the Iraqi family to be granted temporary protection. His view fits with that of Gabriel, quoted at the beginning of this paper. For both of them, fairness is about reserving protection for those "truly deserving" of it.

Fairness is an important value in the SEM. Hence, a widespread understanding amongst caseworkers, which came up a lot in my material, is that their decision-making should always be fair. In most cases, fairness is equated with legal equality. The principle of legal equality means treating equal things equally and unequal things unequally. Therefore, for SEM officials, making fair decisions means using "the same standards for evaluating each claim" (Nora, superior, interview transcript). Ideally, they said, it should not matter who decides a particular case, the outcome should always be the same. For them, the way to achieve this is by strictly following the rules set by institutional practice (see also Lavanchy 2013: 69). Strict rule-following or "law application" is understood in this sense: if there are legal arguments for rejecting a case, it must be rejected. One should not grant asylum or temporary protection in such cases ("just") because making a positive decision might be quicker than meticulously arguing a negative decision, because one has become emotionally attached to the applicant, or because of personal political opinions, for example. At the same time, if there are clearly no justifications for rejecting a claim, reasons should not be made up out of thin air. That too is considered unfair. Connected to this norm of strict rule following is caseworkers' understanding that good decision-makers who properly fulfil their duties "dig deep" into every case to make sure that there are "truly no reasons" for rejection.

Consequently, decision-makers who take justice into their own hands by trying to help someone who is "undeserving" are portrayed as behaving in an unfair and unprofessional manner. Often such behaviour is equated with being "political". One caseworker, Lucy, once explained to me that trying to help an "undeserving" applicant – even someone who had suffered great injustice, for example, by being "so poor he could not feed his five kids" – would be unfair to others because:

This can rapidly lead to one marching to a different drummer. And in my opinion, then you are not being *fair* anymore, even though you want to be. Because your decisions don't conform with our asylum practice, you're not maintaining a *unité de doctrine*. [...] It is not up to us to decide what is *just* or not. [...]. Really, it's the politician who should ask himself that question" (Lucy, caseworker, interview transcript).

As we see, Lucy fears that by "over-generously" helping one person she might end up being "unfair" towards other (more "deserving") asylum seekers. While for her (like most of my other interaction partners) good and professional decision-making is very much linked with fairness, it has little or nothing to do with justice. The world is an unjust place, several of them offered in explanation, but it was not up to them to change that. Justice, they felt, was the responsibility of politics and politicians.[13]

Yet this does not mean that decision-makers never deviate from "strict rule-following". Even where there are reasons for rejection, decisions to grant asylum or temporary protection are sometimes still made. In "exceptional cases", I was told by several interaction partners, it was sometimes okay to turn a blind eye. The expression "to turn a blind eye", used in this context, once again highlights that good decision-making filters out the "undeserving" by finding legal reasons and arguments to exclude them from protection. Only in "exceptional cases" are these reasons deliberately overlooked. As the following quote shows, whether or not decision-makers turn a blind eye and become more lenient may also depend on the ethics of the office:

> You know, if you have a single man without family and you think what he is telling you could possibly be predominantly credible, then you can more easily turn a blind eye. But with someone with a big family back home, you really have to see the *bigger picture* (Julie, caseworker, interview transcript).

Julie and many of her colleagues may therefore turn a blind eye if doing so does not deviate (too much) from their duty to protect the system. She says in the quote that, for a single man, she might stop "digging" for reasons to

---

13 This fits with what Das argues when she writes that "detachment is done by an explicit distancing from the political process, taking it as a given for the particular outcomes to be produced" (2015: 104).

reject the case sooner than for a big family who would all be allowed to stay. That is what she refers to as the "bigger picture". In the latter case, she has to be more careful to reserve the right to stay for those "truly deserving".

The objective and (emotionally) detached decision-maker

Since he has seen so many cases as a superior, he is now able to "see things more clearly, from a certain distance, more objectively", Alberto explains to Rebecca and me. For him distance and objectivity are what it takes to be professional and reach good decisions. He considers Rebecca's decision to be a bad one because it is "too generous". Rebecca thinks that the fact that she was "too nice" and made "too generous" a decision might have been influenced by the family's pleasant appearance when she interviewed them. In other words, she thinks she had liked them too much. In the SEM, emotional attachment and personal involvement are seen as the antithesis of objective decision-making. For a decision to be objective, it should be based solely on the "facts" of the case: on applicants' recorded statements and all the written documents applicants have supplied or decision-makers have acquired. "Distance" is considered crucial for achieving this. In the following, I examine what SEM officials understand by distance, and what measures are undertaken to create distance in order to enable objective decision-making.

SEM officials are not allowed to interview asylum seekers they know personally. If they are assigned the case of an applicant they know, they are obliged to give it back or pass it on to a co-worker. Moreover, in a training module dealing with the role of decision-makers in the interviews, trainees were told to maintain appropriate distance – not just towards asylum seekers, but also towards other professionals who participate in asylum interviews. They were informed that, whereas it was not forbidden to befriend these professionals outside work, the interview was not a place for informal or personal conversation.[14]

---

14 In practice, this is somewhat different. Several decision-makers maintain friendly ties with minute-takers and interpreters and this was evident during interviews when they initiated personal conversations or took breaks together. However, caseworkers are always careful to maintain a certain distance between themselves and the asylum seekers. Thus, conversations between decision-makers and asylum seekers are usually limited to the interview itself and, at times, to some formal small talk on the way to and from the office and the waiting room.

Separate waiting rooms reflect the distance created between different types of actors. At the headquarters, one waiting room is for asylum seekers, and a separate room is shared by interpreters, social aid representatives and other visitors such as myself. At the reception and processing centres where I conducted my fieldwork, these auxiliary personnel sit in the same common room as the decision-makers themselves, while asylum seekers wait elsewhere. This separation ensures that all personal encounters and interactions between officials and asylum seekers are confined to interviews, where they are entirely "professional".

Another feature that promotes professional distance is the seating arrangement during the interviews, which usually take place in an official's personal office. The offices are equipped in a standard manner. The stenographer takes minutes at a desk with a computer. Other participants are placed around a larger rectangular table. These small rooms become very cramped during an interview with five participants (plus me) sitting in them. This forces people to sit close together. Although seating arrangements are generally not conscious decisions, but merely copied from other officials, most decision-makers sit at opposite ends of the table from the asylum seekers, and they therefore sit the farthest apart. When I asked an official why they always sat like that he replied: "Well, for me it's important that I can look the applicant in the eye, that I can look at him during our conversation, that I'm opposite him and sometimes I am also grateful for the distance" (Gabriel, caseworker, interview transcript).

Gabriel's quote points not only to the importance of distance, it also illustrates the value decision-makers ascribe to the "proximity" of face-to-face encounters. Face-to-face encounters are valued for a number of reasons. First, they are seen as an important source of professional-practical knowledge, a term, building on Reckwitz (2003: 289ff), that I use for the institutionalised intuitive knowledge or "gut feeling" that plays an important role in decision-making (see, for instance, Jubany 2011: 86ff; Lavanchy 2014: 92; Macklin 1998).[15] Furthermore, decision-makers believe that by seeing the applicant they can do better justice to the individual case, because they get

---

15 I develop this concept of "professional-practical knowledge" in more detail elsewhere (see Affolter 2017a: 67ff, 2017b: 156ff). It describes what has also been called "tacit knowledge" or *Erfahrungswissen* (experience-based knowledge) by other authors that is acquired *on the job* (see Polanyi 1966; Sofsky & Paris 1995: 54).

a better feeling of what is really at stake. Moreover, many decision-makers told me that it was easier to stand by their decisions if they had personally interviewed the asylum seeker. They usually felt more confident that they were making "the right" decision when this was the case. Finally, one decision-maker told me that she found doing asylum interviews important, because "you sit opposite these people time and again and you realise that it is not just a number [you are dealing with], but a human being with all his hopes and dreams" (Lucy, caseworker, interview transcript). Yet, while close encounters in the interviews are acknowledged as important for the aforementioned reasons, decision-makers also see a danger that, like Rebecca, they will become emotionally attached. All my interaction partners told me that, for this reason, they usually put the case file aside for a couple of days after the interview, to (re-)gain some distance, so that their decision will not be influenced by sentiments the interview triggered. In this way, they become objective again.

As shown above, Lucy felt that it is important not to reduce people to numbers. I frequently encountered this norm in the SEM. Reducing people to numbers, not recognising them as persons (but instead as "piece[s] of paper") is regarded as doing one's job badly. Thus, a common outside critique (of reducing people to numbers, cases or files) is mirrored in this internal value (see, for instance, Eule 2014: 109; Fuglerud 2004: 36; Scheffer 2001).[16] Good decision-makers are supposed to care for the people they deal with (see also Watkins-Hayes 2009: 70).

The sufficiently but not overly suspicious decision-maker

Alberto tells me that over the years he has become "stricter" and "less naïve". Both attributes he (implicitly) connects to fair decision-making: They allow him to be fair. As shown above, the common assumption in the SEM is that most asylum seekers are "bogus". They belong to the group considered "economic migrants" and are trying to manipulate the system in order to stay (see also Kelly 2012: 755; Souter 2011: 48). It is therefore the decision-makers' duty to combat "fraud", uncover the "underserving" and reject their claims

---

16 However, "distancing", as Eule (2014: 109) calls it, also occurs in the SEM in ways that are not recognised and reflected on by caseworkers, for instance, in terms of language usage.

as quickly as possible.[17] This understanding of asylum decision-making leads to "a shift from trying to find the truth to searching for untruth, from a concern with proof to a concern with lies" (Kelly 2012: 765).

On the whole, the role decision-makers have in the interview and in decision-making processes is that of a "sceptic", as some have called it themselves. They see it as their duty to ask as many questions as necessary until they are convinced that the asylum seeker's story is true, or to produce sufficient arguments for writing a negative decision. Similar to what Alpes and Spire (2014: 269) describe for French consulates and Scheffer (2003:456) cites with regard to German asylum administrations, in the SEM "to be suspicious is a sign of professionalism" (Alpes and Spire 2014: 269). Conversely, to believe asylum seekers' statements without testing their credibility is a sign of naïvety. Decision-makers often worry when statements "seem credible" that the asylum seekers memorised them beforehand, or have knowledge about certain things for reasons other than personal persecution. For instance, once, after an asylum interview in which the applicant had talked for quite a long time about being in prison, the decision-maker said to me: "This is maybe a bit 'obsessive' (*zwanghaft*), but the applicant could also have been a prison guard and that's why he's so familiar with the conditions in prison" (field notes).

While being sceptical is a sign of professionalism, being overly suspicious is regarded as a vice. As Das argues, (emotional) detachment does not equal cold disinterest (2015: 103ff; see also Candea et al. 2015: 24). In the SEM, disinterested or indifferent decision-makers are called "cynics". They are criticised – mostly behind their backs, as far as I observed – for doing their job badly.[18] Cynics are said to enter asylum interviews with closed minds,

---

17 The same has been observed in the case of registry offices in Switzerland and welfare offices in the US (Lavanchy 2014: 99; Watkins-Hayes 2009: 50f).

18 An observation I made in the SEM is that decision-makers often denounce their colleagues – particularly those working in other units of the office – for bad decision-making (see Affolter et al. 2019). The most common emic distinction made is between "hardliners" and "softies" (see Miaz 2017: 372). While the former are criticised for being too rigid in their decision-making, the latter are accused of being too lenient. During my fieldwork, I only observed such criticism being made behind other people's backs. However, I was privy to a rumour which leads me to believe that the different "attitudes" may actually be used in apportioning cases. I was told that superiors tend to direct the applications they think will most likely be rejected to those caseworkers who take negative decisions more frequently than others whereas the cases more likely to be judged favourably are

always already knowing that everything will be a lie. This opposes the norm of open-mindedness. During my research, I was frequently told what is also taught in the training modules, that decision-makers must be open-minded in order to do their job well. They should go into every interview with a *tabula rasa* even if, at the same time, they should already have an idea of what the decision might be in order to conduct the interview efficiently.

While becoming a cynic is perceived as a greater risk for older employees who have already "seen too much", being naïve (and not sceptical enough) is regarded as an attribute that new employees have to grow out of. Connected to these perceptions is a crucial difference in critique. Whereas naïve decision-making is regularly equated with being *unprofessional*, I have never come across that criticism of cynical decision-making.[19] New decision-makers who "naïvely believe everything the claimants tell them" appear to lack sufficient understanding of what it means to properly fulfil their duty, and experienced decision-makers who naïvely believe an applicant are often criticised as being lazy – too lazy, one could interpret, to properly fulfil their duties. On the other hand, the term often used to describe an overly suspicious and cynical attitude is *déformation professionelle*, or occupational hazard. Used by SEM officials to describe how the views of decision-makers may become distorted by long service on the job, this term is applied when veracity is disparaged too much.[20] Thus, critiques of cynical decision-making do not criticise officials for being unprofessional or not protecting the system, but for taking protection too far, and losing sight of those who are "deserving".

The apolitical decision-maker

When Alberto, slightly defensively, brought up "the question of nation states" in a conversation introduced earlier in the chapter, and "whether one thinks nation states are good or not," he was referring to a particular political ide-

---

given to those decision-makers with a reputation for granting asylum more readily (see also Fassin and Kobelinsky 2012: 462).

19 And neither have Jonathan Miaz and Ephraim Poertner who also conducted research in the SEM (see Affolter et al. 2019: 281).

20 In academia, the term *déformation professionelle* can be traced back to the sociologist Daniel Warnotte, who used it to describe how "bureaucrats" become "intellectually and emotionally damaged by their roles" (Maccoby 2007: 62).

ology that questions the fundamental idea of nation states. Even if he was sympathetic towards this idea – Alberto did not really state his opinion and left this possibility open – the message he conveyed is clear: On the job, there is no place for personal political opinions. But not only that. By saying that these problems "cannot be solved by what we do", he insinuated that decision-making is also apolitical. Both of these statements reflect perspectives that are common in the SEM.

The "apolitical" norm fits with the impersonal spirit Weber depicts as an important feature of the bureaucratic ethos. He writes:

> "*Sine ira et studio*," without hatred or passion, and hence without affection or enthusiasm. The dominant norms are concepts of straightforward duty without regard to personal considerations. [...] This is the spirit in which the ideal official conducts his office (2013: 225).

In contrast, the "politician's element" is "*ira et studium*" (Weber 1991: 95). Thus, according to Weber, politicians must have passion and fight, whereas bureaucrats should do neither. A similar opinion is widespread in the SEM: there "all" an official should do is to follow rules and "neutrally apply the law". This is illustrated in the following quote:

> I have a problem with "missionaries". And there are some here in the SEM. We don't have a mission here. We just have to decide upon cases. We don't have to protect Switzerland from foreigners. That is not our role. But some people here feel this way. They think that there are too many asylum seekers here. But that is not my problem. I am paid to take decisions, so I take decisions. On the other hand, there are some who proselytise on behalf of the asylum seekers. They think that everybody should be able to stay here. But that is not the case. We have the law. [...] And then there are the others who say: "If you give a temporary permit to this guy, who is only 20, and then he stays for 30 years, that will cost Switzerland 10 million francs." Again, that is not my problem. If he fulfils the eligibility criteria he can stay. If you're not happy with it, you have to change the law. But then you have to go into politics, you shouldn't be working here. (Barbara, caseworker, interview transcript)

I find Barbara's quote particularly telling in three regards. First, she depicts "doing the job one is paid to do" and "sticking to the rules" as apolitical work.

However, from an analytical perspective, I would not claim that SEM decision-makers are apolitical actors, but rather that they make policies (and politics) while "translating and implementing [them] into action" (Wedel et al. 2005: 34). Barbara's statement illustrates how "the political" is masked "under the cloak of neutrality" (Shore and Wright 1997: 8).

Second, Barbara uses the word "missionaries" to describe a role decision-makers should not take on. Missionaries pursue clear goals with their decision-making: they either want to enable everybody to stay, or to make sure that as few people as possible are allowed to remain in Switzerland. In contrast, Barbara claims that a professional decision-maker's only aim should be to "correctly" and "neutrally" apply the law. For her, professional decision-making has no room for ideologies and pursuit of goals other than following the law. At first sight this could be perceived to contradict what I have described as being the ethics of the office. But I argue that this is not so for the following reason. Although my interaction partners rarely presented what I have described as the ethics of the office as explicit norms, they are, nevertheless, prevalent in my material as ideologies underlying the explicitly stated norms and values. Because they lie at the heart of professionalism in the SEM, these ideologies (unlike the ones Barbara describes) are not perceived by decision-makers as being outside the law, but they implicitly inform what "correct" and "neutral" rule-following means.

Third, Barbara's quote tellingly advocates for "political neutrality" – which is widely recognised as an important norm within the SEM. However, what this means exactly may vary for individual decision-makers. At several points during our conversations, Barbara clearly identified herself as "anti-SVP" (the right-wing Swiss People's Party). Hence, she was most critical of what she sometimes called "SVP-decision-making". On the other hand, several other interaction partners criticised "left-wing decision-making". For example, one superior claimed that some of her "left-wing" colleagues, who were too lenient in their decision-making because they "want[ed] to save the world", were egoistic. By calling her "left-wing" colleagues' decision-making egoistic, she is criticising them for doing what feels good and looking out for themselves, instead of strictly following the rules. In her view, they should have fulfilled their duties as decision-makers by attending to the broader aims of the office: protecting the system and reserving government protection for the "truly deserving".

The necessity of "digging deep"

This section addresses a widespread decision-making practice regarded as a "correct" and "neutral" rule application: "digging deep". My example shows how the ethics of the office shapes decision-makers' discretionary practices, making it normal and desirable for them to act in specific ways. I understand discretionary practices to be processes of interpreting the law when fitting it to specific cases or situations. Therefore, discretion necessarily forms part of the law, since (written) law is "by its very nature unspecific" and "always needs to be applied to a specific situation, and therefore interpreted" (Eckert 2015: 1). "Digging deep" is a discretionary practice used to "apply" Article 7 of the Swiss Asylum Act, which regulates "proof of refugee status".[21] The example of "digging deep" that follows allows me to show how this everyday practice is shaped by the norms discussed above, and also how it reaffirms these same norms and values, upon which it is based.

Fair decision-making requires strict rule-following. As discussed above, if legal arguments support rejecting a case, it must be rejected. Many scholars have observed that asylum proceedings function as quests to find reasons to doubt applicants and deny their claims (see, for instance, Scheffer 2001: 194, 2003: 455). This can be seen in asylum interviews, where questioning is oriented towards "discovering" mistakes and "uncovering untruths". While decision-makers simply call this practice "testing credibility", I call it "digging deep". When "digging deep", decision-makers ask "tricky" questions in asylum interviews and/or undertake extra investigations until they have enough arguments to reject a claim, or are convinced that the applicant's story is true "after all".[22]

As the above-mentioned norms and values suggest, "digging deep" is the epitome of good and professional decision-making in the SEM. The practice

---

21 Article 7 AsylA reads as follows: "1Any person who applies for asylum must prove or at least credibly demonstrate their refugee status. 2Refugee status is credibly demonstrated if the authority regards it as proven on the balance of probabilities. 3Cases are not credible in particular if they are unfounded in essential points or are inherently contradictory, do not correspond to the facts or are substantially based on forged or falsified evidence" (https://www.admin.ch/opc/en/classified-compilation/19995092/index.html [accessed 20 September 2018].

22 An exception is when decision-makers know "from the beginning" that a story is "simply true" due to their professional-practical knowledge (see footnote 15).

is framed as "necessary", allowing decision-makers to make positive asylum decisions with a "clear conscience":

> Sometimes you do an additional interview when technically everything indicates that a story could be true but there are two, three contradictions in it. In such cases it just *feels strange* to grant asylum when there are still some uncertainties, some open questions. So, then you do [an additional interview] so that if you then get an answer that really satisfies you, you can write a positive decision *with a clear conscience*. (Denise, caseworker, interview transcript)

Here Denise is talking about the need to carry out additional asylum interviews if, after the first "in-depth" interview, too many uncertainties remain. She refers to cases in which something "feels off", but there are not enough discrepancies to reject the claim. In those cases, Denise declares, she has to "dig deep" in order to see whether there are arguments against asylum. If arguments exist, the claim "can" be rejected. If not, a positive decision can be made with a "clear conscience".

In order to "dig deep", decision-makers use a particular questioning technique taught to all caseworkers during their initial training.[23] It is common for decision-makers to begin their questioning by asking about applicants' reasons for leaving their country and applying for asylum. Interviews open with a question such as: "Why did you leave country and apply for asylum in Switzerland?" After that, decision-makers follow-up with specific "wh-questions" and some yes or no questions. At the end of the interview, the asylum seekers are usually confronted with contradictions found in their story.

The open question at the beginning is intended to give asylum seekers the opportunity to tell their stories. One purpose of the follow-up questions (the wh- questions in particular) then is to enable the decision-makers to collect all the necessary information for taking their decisions (e.g. who exactly the persecutors were and what might have been motives for persecution). Another purpose of these questions is to see whether asylum seeker can talk in detail about certain events they are asked about (e.g. "please tell me in detail about the daily routine in prison") or to generate answers the decision-makers can then compare with "facts" they can look up (e.g. "what was

---

23 For a closer discussion of this technique in reference to a specific empirical example, see Affolter (2017a: 71ff).

the name of your church that was bombed?"). Both these things – depending on whether asylum seekers manage to answer them adequately or not – serve as indicators of credibility or non-credibility. Finally, these questions allow for comparisons. Hence, in order to "be able to" reason non-credibility decisions on the basis of contradictions, decision-makers need on-file facts that they can compare with each other.

My interaction partners used two distinct metaphors to describe this three-step questioning technique: "It is like a funnel (*Trichter*)", one of them said. Another one compared it to the "tightening of a noose (*Zuziehen einer Schlinge*)". The first metaphor seems to indicate that one gets closer and closer to the heart of the matter through this kind of questioning, "the truth" (or "non-truth") of what happened. The second metaphor seems to assume that asylum seekers often lie, and sees the procedure as a means of exposing the liars. Several decision-makers stated that starting with an open question was useful because asylum seekers' "free narrative" (*freien Erzählung*) tended to get tangled up in contradictions "if the story was not true".

As Scheffer (2001: 184) and Trueman (2009: 296) have argued, such questioning techniques, rather than passively "discovering" mistakes and "untruths", actively generate them. They therefore contribute to creating the figure of the "false refugee". Once asylum seekers have been classified as "false refugees" and assigned to the legal category of "non-refugee" (with or without temporary admission), their very existence reinforces the perception that there "are" indeed many false refugees. This perception, in turn, strengthens endeavours to identify and deny them asylum (see also Zimmermann 2011: 337). Thus, the practice of "digging deep" reaffirms decision-makers' duty to protect the system, and confirms ideas of how professionals should act in service of this duty (see Eckert, this volume).

Concluding remarks

In this chapter, I have shown how the ethics of protecting the system make "digging deep" the routine thing for decision-makers to do. "Digging deep", in turn, reinforces the professional norms that lie at its heart, and reaffirms decision-makers' role as protectors of the system. By exploring the professional norm of fairness in detail, I have portrayed how the procedural values that make up the bureaucratic ethos are shaped by the ethics of the office. The bureaucratic ethics not only seem to yield professionally necessary behaviours – things decision-makers *have to* do – certain professional behaviours, such as "digging deep", also become *morally right* or, we could also say, *ethical* ways for decision-makers to act.

It has frequently been argued that "bureaucracies" and "bureaucrats" are indifferent (see Arendt 2013; Bauman 2000; Gill 2016; Herzfeld 1992). Gill thus writes that "bureaucrats" cease to care about the people they deal with because their concern and compassion for them is overridden by other concerns: most notably instrumental-rational rule-following (2016: 136). However, I have shown on the basis of the procedural norm of fairness not how concern for people is overridden by other concerns but rather how it is brought into accordance with the exclusionary ethics of the office.

For this purpose, many authors have argued that in order to understand how bureaucrats bring in line law and policy work, we need to pay attention to "bureaucrats'" actions, routines and habits (Fassin 2015: 4; Silbey 2005: 324; Wedel et al. 2005: 34). Here, rather than "simply" looking at what "bureaucrats" do, I have dealt with one important aspect of *what makes them do what they do*; namely, what they think they should do (see Eckert, this volume).

Institutional norms shape the "practices of the state" (Migdal and Schlichte 2005: 15; see also Bierschenk & Olivier de Sardan 2014: 5ff; Eckert et al. 2012: 15). Such norms, images of what the public good constitutes and the understanding of how the public good might best be served change over time (Eckert, this volume). Taking what bureaucrats think they should be doing seriously at different times and places, i.e. within their specific historical situations, we are able to show how bureaucratic ethics and ethos are transformed. This allows us to better understand "states at work" (Bierschenk and Olivier de Sardan 2014) in and across different (historical) settings. My analysis offers an explanation for the exclusionary workings of the Swiss state, asylum law and policies. In particular, it contributes to understanding why the majority of asylum claims end up being rejected on the basis of "non-credibility".

Bibliography

Affolter, Laura. 2017a. Protecting the System: Decision-Making in a Swiss Asylum Administration. *PhD Dissertation* (unpublished). Bern: University of Bern.

Affolter, Laura. 2017b. Asyl-Verwaltung kraft Wissen: Die Herstellung von Entscheidungswissen in einer Schweizer Asylbehörde. In: Christian Lahusen and Stephanie Schneider, eds, *Asyl verwalten. Zur bürokratischen Bearbeitung eines gesellschaftlichen Problems*. Bielefeld: transcript: 145–171.

Affolter, Laura. 2018. "Der grösste Teil von [unserem] Job ist Unglaubhaftigkeit". *Terra Cognita*, 32: 92–94.

Affolter, Laura, Jonathan Miaz and Ephraim Poertner. 2019. Taking the "Just" Decision. Caseworkers and their Communities of Interpretation in a Swiss Asylum Office. In: Nick Gill and Anthony Good, eds, *Asylum Determination in Europe: Ethnographic Perspectives*. Basingstoke: Palgrave Macmillan. 263–283.

Alpes, Maybritt Jill and Alexis Spire. 2014. Dealing with Law in Migration Control: The Powers of Street-Level Bureaucrats at French Consulates. *Social & Legal Studies* 23(2): 261–274.

Arendt, Hannah 2013: *Eichmann in Jerusalem: Ein Bericht von der Banalität des Bösen*. München: Piper.

Asylum Act, (AsylA), of 26 June 1998 (Status as of 1 January 2018). 142.31.

Bauman, Zygmunt. 2000 (1989). *Modernity and the Holocaust*. Ithaca: Cornell University Press.

Bierschenk, Thomas and Jean-Pierre Olivier de Sardan. 2014. Studying the Dynamics of African Bureaucracies: An Introduction to States at Work. In: Thomas Bierschenk and Jean-Pierre Olivier de Sardan, eds, *States at Work: Dynamics of African Bureaucracies*. Leiden, Boston: Brill: 3–33.

Bourdieu, Pierre. 1976. *Entwurf einer Theorie der Praxis auf der ethnologischen Grundlage der kabylischen Gesellschaft*. Frankfurt am Main: Suhrkamp.

Cabot, Heath. 2013. The Social Aesthetics of Eligibility: NGO Aid and Indeterminacy in the Greek Asylum Process. *American Ethnologist* 40(3): 452–466.

Candea, Matei, Joanna Cook, Catherine Trundle and Thomas Yarrow. 2015. Introduction: Reconsidering Detachment. In: Matei Candea, Joanna Cook, Catherine Trundle and Thomas Yarrow, eds, *Detachment. Essays on the Limits of Relational Thinking*. Manchester: Manchester University Press: 1–31.

Convention on the Rights of the Child, adopted and opened for signature, ratification and accession by General Assembly resolution 44/25 of 20 November 1989, entry into force 2 September 1990, in accordance with article 49.

Convention relating to the Status of Refugees, adopted on 28 July 1951 by the United Nations Conference of Plenipotentiaries on the Status of Refugees and Stateless Persons convened under General Assembly resolution 429 (V) of 14 December 1950, entry into force: 22 April 1954, in accordance with article 43.

Crawley, Heaven. 1999. *Breaking Down the Barriers: A Report on the Conduct of Asylum Interviews at Ports*. London: Immigration Law Practitioners' Association (ILPA).

Däpp, Heinz 1984: Bankrott einer staatspolitischen Maxime. In: Heinz Däpp and Rudolf Karlen, eds, *Asylpolitik gegen Flüchtlinge*. Basel: Lenos: 211–226.

Das, Veena. 2015. Professionalism and Expertise: Comment. In: Matei Candea, Joanna Cook, Catherine Trundle and Thomas Yarrow, eds, *Detachment. Essays on the Limits of Relational Thinking*. Manchester: Manchester University Press: 102–111.

Eckert, Julia. 2015. *Summary of Workshop on Ethos and Ethics in Migration Bureaucracies* (unpublished manuscript).

Eckert, Julia, Andrea Behrends and Andreas Dafinger. 2012. Governance – and the State: An Anthropological Approach. *Ethnoscripts* 14(1): 14–34.

Eule, Tobias. 2014. *Inside Immigration Law. Migration Management and Policy Application in Germany*. Farnham: Ashgate.

Fassin, Didier. 2007. Humanitarianism as a Politics of Life. *Public Culture* 19(3): 499–520.

Fassin, Didier. 2013. The Precarious Truth of Asylum. *Public Culture* 25(1): 39–63.

Fassin, Didier. 2015. Introduction: Governing Precarity. In: Didier Fassin, ed., *At the Heart of the State. The Moral World of Institutions*. London: Pluto Press. ix–xi.

Fassin, Didier. 2016. *From Right to Favor: The Refugee Question as Moral Crisis*. https://www.thenation.com/article/from-right-to-favor/ [accessed 28 September 2018].

Fassin, Didier and Carolina Kobelinsky. 2012. How Asylum Claims Are Adjudicated: The Institution as a Moral Agent. *Revue française de sociologie* 53(4): 444–472.

Fuglerud, Oivind. 2004. Constructing Exclusion: The Micro-Sociology of an Immigration Department. *Social Anthropology* 12(1): 25–40.

Gill, Nick. 2009. Presentational State Power: Temporal and Spacial Influences over Asylum Sector Decisionmakers. *Transactions of the Institute of British Geographers* 34(2): 215–233.

Gill, Nick. 2016. *Nothing Personal: Geographies of Governing and Activism in the British Asylum System*. Oxford: Wiley-Blackwell.

Graeber, David. 2015. *The Utopia of Rules: On Technology, Stupidity, and the Secret Joys of Bureaucracy*. Brooklyn, London: Melville House.

Harvey, Colin. 1997. Restructuring Asylum: Recent Trends in United Kingdom Asylum Law and Policy. *International Journal of Refugee Law* 9(1): 60–73.

Herzfeld, Michael. 1992. *The Social Production of Indifference: Exploring the Symbolic Roots of Western Bureaucracy*. New York: Berg.

Heyman, Josiah McC. 2009. Trust, Privilege, and Discretion in the Governance of US Borderlands with Mexico. *Canadian Journal of Law and Society* 24(3): 367–390.

Jubany, Olga. 2011. Constructing Truths in a Culture of Disbelief: Understanding Asylum Screening from Within. *International Sociology* 26(1): 74–94.

Jubany, Olga. 2017. *Screening Asylum in a Culture of Disbelief: Truths, Denials and Sceptical Borders*. Cham: Palgrave Macmillan.

Kelly, Tobias. 2012. Sympathy and Suspicion: Torture, Asylum, and Humanity. *Journal of the Royal Anthropological Institute* 18(4): 753–768.

Kobelinsky, Carolina. 2015. In Search of Truth: How Asylum Applications Are Adjudicated. In: Didier Fassin, ed., *At the Heart of the State: The Moral World of Institutions*. London: Pluto Press: 67–92.

Lavanchy, Anne. 2013 L'amour aux services de l'état civil: régulations institutionnelles de l'intimité et fabrique de la resemblance nationale en Suisse. *Migrations Société* 150: 61–77.

Lavanchy, Anne. 2014. Die Gefühlswelt des Gesetzes. Die kritische Umsetzung von eherechtlichen Vorschriften im Zivistandsamt. *FAMPRA* 1: 92–117.

Lavanchy, Anne and Elodie Garros (forthcoming). Ouvrir, traiter et clore les dossiers: écriture et évaluation. In: Anne Lavanchy, Pascal Mahon, Flora DiDonato, Elodie Garros and Tania Zittoun, eds, *La Fabrique de l'intégration*. Lausanne: Antipodes (2019).

Lipsky, Michael. 2010. *Street-Level Bureaucracy, 30th anniversary Edition: Dilemmas of the Individual in Public Service*. New York: Russel Sage Foundation.

Marfleet, Philip. 2006. *Refugees in a Global Era*. Basingstoke: Palgrave.

Maccoby, Michael. 2007. *The Leaders We Need: And What Makes Us Follow*. Boston: Harvard Business School Press.

Macklin, Audrey. 1998. *Truth and Consequences: Credibility Determination in the Refugee Context*. Conference paper. Ottawa: International Association of Refugee Law Judges. http://refugeestudies.org/UNHCR/97 - Truth and Consequences. Credibility Determination in Refugee Context. by Audrey Macklin.pdf [accessed 28 September 2018].

Miaz, Jonathan. 2017. *Politique d'asile et sophistication du droit: Pratiques administratives et défense juridique desmigrants en Suisse (1981-2015)*. PhD Dissertation (unpublished). Lausanne: Université de Lausanne and Université de Strasbourg.

Migdal, Joel S. and Klaus Schlichte. 2005. Rethinking the State. In: Klaus Schlichte, ed., *The Dynamics of States. The Formation and Crisis of State Domination*. Aldershot: Ashgate: 1–40.

Piguet, Etienne. 2006. *Einwanderungsland Schweiz: Fünf Jahrzehnte halb geöffnete Grenzen*. Bern: Haupt.

Poertner, Ephraim. 2017. Governing Asylum through Configurations of Productivity and Deterrence: Effects on the Spatiotemporal Trajectories of Cases in Switzerland. *Geoforum* 78: 12–21.

Polanyi, Michael. 1966. *The Tacit Dimension*. Chicago: University of Chicago Press.

Reckwitz, Andreas. 2003: Grundelemente einer Theorie sozialer Praktiken: Eine sozialtheoretische Perspektive. *Zeitschrift für Soziologie* 32(4): 282–301.

Sbriccoli, Tommaso and Stefano Jacoviello. 2011. The Case of S: Elaborating the "Right" Narrative to Fit Normative/Political Expectations in Asylum Procedure in Italy. In: Livia Holden, ed., *Cultural Expertise and Litigation*. Abingdon, New York: Routledge: 172–194.

Scheffer, Thomas. 2001. *Asylgewährung: Eine ethnographische Analyse des deutschen Asylverfahrens*. Stuttgart: Lucius & Lucius.

Scheffer, Thomas. 2003. Kritik der Urteilskraft: Wie die Asylprüfung Unentscheidbares in Entscheidbares überführt. In: Jochen Oltmer, ed.,

Migration steuern und verwalten: Deutschland vom späten 19. Jahrhundert bis zur Gegenwart. Göttingen: Vandenhoeck & Ruprecht: 423–458.

Shore, Cris, and Susan Wright. 1997. Introduction: Policy: A New Field of Anthropology. In: Cris Shore and Susan Wright, eds, *Anthropology of Policy: Critical Perspectives on Governance and Power*. London, New York: Routledge: 3–30.

Shore, Cris and Susan Wright. 2011. Conceptualising Policy: Technologies of Governance and the Politics of Visibility. In: Cris Shore, Susan Wright and Davide Però, eds, *Policy Worlds: Anthropology and the Analysis of Contemporary Power*. New York: Berghahn Books: 1–25.

Silbey, Susan S. 2005. After Legal Consciousness. *Annual Review of Law and Social Science* 1: 323–368.

Sofsky, Wolfgang, and Rainer Paris. 1994. *Figurationen sozialer Macht: Autorität, Stellvertretung, Koalition*. Frankfurt a.M.: Suhrkamp.

Souter, James. 2011. A Culture of Disbelief or Denial? Critiquing Refugee Status Determination in the United Kingdom. *Oxford Monitor of Forced Migration* 1(1): 48–59.

Staatssekretariat für Migration SEM. *Handbuch Asyl und Rückkehr: Artikel C5 Der Nachweis der Flüchtlingseigenschaft*. https://www.sem.admin.ch/dam/data/sem/asyl/verfahren/hb/c/hb-c5-d.pdf [accessed 28 September 2018].

Terdiman, Richard. 1987. The Force of Law: Toward a Sociology of the Juridical Field by Pierre Bourdieu: Translator's Introduction. *Hastings Law Journal* 38(5): 805–853.

Ticktin, Miriam. 2006. Where Ethics and Politics Meet: The Violence of Humanitarianism in France. *American Ethnologist* 33(1): 33–49.

Trueman, Trevor. 2009. Reasons for Refusal: An Audit of 200 Refusals of Ethiopian Asylum-Seekers in England. *Journal of Immigration, Asylum and Nationality Law* 23(3): 281–308.

Watkins-Hayes, Celeste. 2009. *The New Welfare Bureaucrats. Entanglements of Race, Class, and Policy Reform*. Chicago: University of Chicago Press.

Weber, Max. 1991 (1948). *From Max Weber: Essays in Sociology*. Translated, edited and with an introduction by Hans H. Gerth and C. Wright Mills. London, New York: Routledge and Kegan Paul.

Weber, Max. 2013 (1978). *Economy and Society* (edited by Guenther Roth and Claus Wittich). Berkeley: University of California Press.

Wedel, Janine R., Cris Shore, Gregory Feldman and Stacey Lathrop. 2005. Toward an Anthropology of Public Policy. *Annals of the American Academy of Political and Social Science* 600(1): 30–51.

Zetter, Roger. 2007. More Labels, Fewer Refugees: Remaking the Refugee Label in an Era of Globalization. *Journal of Refugee Studies* 20(2): 172–192.

Zimmermann, Susan E. 2011. Reconsidering the Problem of "Bogus" Refugees with "Socio-economic Motivations" for Seeking Asylum. *Mobilities* 6: 335–352.

The Asylum Procedure in Border Detention
The Technicalities and Morals of Truth Determination in France

Chowra Makaremi

Introduction

France has established a border control system at airports that organizes deportations in real time. These deportation practices are nonetheless restricted by international laws concerning asylum, which the French state undertook to respect as a signatory to the 1951 Geneva Convention on the Protection of Refugees. Two principles apply in particular: an asylum seeker is exempt from presenting documents to cross the border of a country where he or she seeks asylum, and he or she cannot be deported until his or her application has been heard and examined.[1] At Roissy-CdG Airport in Paris, for example, asylum seekers must be detained until their applications can be examined and adjudicated before they are allowed to enter France. Thus, the legalities of refugee protection necessitate their detention. This places asylum administration at the origins of border detention (Crépeau 1995).

State power holds sway over asylum applicants in an exceptional legal and administrative space determined by specific identification and classification processes. An applicant's personal account, given to a refugee protection agent at his or her hearing, is the foundation of asylum procedure. The conditions of migration are negotiated in a space where the national host community is redefined literally by filtering and excluding those who do not belong to it, and figuratively by affirming common rationalities and

---

1 "Non-refoulement" (defined in article 33 of the 1951 Convention Relating to the Status of Refugees) has become a principle of *customary* international law, as it applies even to states that are not parties to this Convention or its 1967 Protocol.

moral values, such as democratic assistance or protection of the welfare state against abuses and false refugees (Noiriel 1992, Crépeau 1995, Lavenex 1999, Schuster 2005). Several studies have pointed out that asylum management in Western countries is based on truth determination practices (Herlihy, Gleeson and Turner 2010, Fassin 2013, Kobelinsky 2015, Kynsileto and Puumala 2015, Maskens 2015). These practices are articulated from imperatives of control that aim to restrict the immigration of asylum seekers from unwanted populations (Marrus 1985, Belorgey 2003 and 2007, Rousseau and Foxen 2006, Valluy 2009). These studies remind us that rules established (or crafted *in situ*) for truth determination are inseparable from issues of speech, power and population management. Starting with my fieldwork narratives, this chapter explores how asylum procedures at the border, built on ways of determining truth and falsehood, are exercised under the mutual suspicion of both the applicants and the administration.

For someone experiencing detention at the border, control and resistance are tied to the process of "narrating oneself" (Butler 2005), of putting memory into words. But this personal narrative is conditioned by the applicant's precarious situation and by administrative scepticism. Narrative structure and form are anchored in the narrator's psychic, cultural and social condition, including his or her experience of border detention. Both sides have a stake in how the narrative is articulated.

For applicants, coherence and veracity determine the likelihood of sincerity and whether their cases fit under an increasingly restrictive reading of the Geneva Convention. Narratives must also confront, deflect or decode collective representations in the host country that "produce indifference" towards asylum seekers (Herzfeld 199) in the administrative world of border control. For the administration, standards of judgement perform the double work of narrative transcription and evaluation, constructing a "regime of verification" (Foucault 2004b) to determine the fate of refuges. This chapter will investigate processes of identification and administrative categorization, the interactions and narratives that together build asylum procedure as a space where "truth" is investigated by asking: What epistemology is at work here? What meanings and definitions of "truth" apply? How are national rationalities and moral order delineated at the border, where individual decisions control who can enter and who cannot?

This chapter explores these questions through an ethnography of border detention based on my fieldwork at Roissy-CDG Airport in Paris, where

I volunteered as a legal assistant with the NGO Anafé (*Assistance nationales aux frontières pour les étrangers*) between 2004 and 2008. I assisted undocumented migrants and asylum seekers with their paperwork and helped them navigate their administrative journey through border detention. This "observatory participation" (Makaremi 2008) not only gave me access to the detention centre, it helped me understand the procedure, its temporality, its actors, its spoken and unspoken rules and how it functions in general. This kind of engaged ethnography presented specific methodological and ethical challenges. But it also offered new paths for knowledge production that combine the traditional demands of objectivity with an openness to the heuristics of emotions, experience and empathy.[2] The analysis I offer here builds on field notes, observations of individual trajectories, a critical review of forty-eight asylum decisions and interviews with both refugee protection officers and former detainees who had been admitted to France. Many years have passed since I collected this empirical data. Almost a dozen laws and regulations have modified border detention and asylum procedure in France. However, these legislative changes did not address real needs for procedural readjustment but rather directly reflect the role of immigration in global political power struggles. A new modality of ill-treatment and exclusion through administrative complexity has instilled institutional violence in the rule of law. Nevertheless, here I focus on the underlying logics and administrative episteme, setting aside recent border detention and asylum controversies, which have rearranged but not substantially affected the form of government at play.[3]

The bureaucracy of border asylum

According to figures from the French Ministry of the Interior, 33 percent of those kept in airport waiting zones in 2015 were asylum seekers (Anafé 2016). The special procedure for examining asylum applications in such areas has evolved over the past three decades, but its guiding principle is as follows: applications are examined at the border by officials of the Asylum Division, who draw up "opinions" for the Ministry of the Interior, which decides

---

2 I discuss these issues in Makaremi 2008.
3 For a discussion of recent developments of asylum laws see, for instance, Palluel 2016.

whether or not to admit the asylum seekers to France. Yet, this decision is only a first screening. Although the administrative authority is the same, asylum at the border is treated differently from asylum within in country. Several procedural differences at the border influence the trajectories of asylum seekers.

Firstly, application at the border is not for refugee status, but to gain admission to the country as an asylum seeker. Once an asylum seeker's application has been accepted, he or she is allowed to leave the waiting area and enter France, but must apply for asylum in the prefecture within eight days. His or her application, consisting of a written form and an oral interview, is reviewed for the purpose of granting refugee status by the French Agency for the Protection of Refugees and Stateless Persons (OFPRA).[4] It is not rare for an asylum seeker admitted to the country to be subsequently rejected by OFPRA and then by the National Court of Asylum (CNDA), which examines appeals made by rejected applicants (Valluy 2009). Conversely, an asylum seeker rejected at the border, but who succeeds in entering France at the end of his or her stay in the waiting zone, can still apply for asylum and obtain refugee status.

Secondly, asylum application at the border does not involve the filling out of a form or presentation of a written personal narrative. The examination is based solely on an oral hearing lasting between ten minutes and three hours; the determination is reported within three days of the hearing on average.[5] OFPRA's procedure for granting refugee status allows the asylum seeker one month to complete a written file in French, which may be followed by an oral interview. According to OFPRA's 2015 annual report, the average time it took to process an application was 100 days – reducing processing time has been an important political issue in immigration control policy (OFPRA 2015: 35). Finally, OFPRA agents at the border examine asylum applications under Geneva Convention rules only: no subsidiary protection can be granted at the border, although this can happen on French territory.[6] Although offi-

---

4   Karen Akoka offers a sociological history of this institution (Akoka 2019).
5   "In 2015, 72% of OFPRA's decisions were given within 48 hours of placement in the waiting zone, and 90% within 96 hours". (OFPRA 2016)
6   In France, subsidiary protection is the protection granted to claimants who are not granted official refugee protection (for instance, only subsidiary protection can be granted to people coming from countries officially recognized as "safe countries" by OFPRA, such as Turkey).

cials assert that examination criteria are the same in the waiting area and on French soil,[7] the Asylum Division at the border works according to particular rules (spoken and unspoken) linked to the specificities and technicalities of border detention. At the same time, the issues at stake and the practices of asylum treatment in a restricted space and time can be seen as a microcosm of asylum as a whole, as this chapter explores.

In 1991, the Marchand Decree established the procedure by which asylum seekers in waiting areas at the border are heard. The procedure falls within the competence of the Border Asylum Division (DAF), which was originally attached to the Foreign Ministry. In 1998, applications increased considerably, coming close to current figures.[8] In addition to a permanent staff of four OFPRA protection officers, ten to fifteen contractors were recruited and trained to handle the increase in applications by the head of the Sub-Directorate of Refugees at the Ministry of Foreign Affairs. This coincided with the introduction of a more restrictive doctrine for granting asylum.[9] From 1998 until 2001, the first team of agents left the DAF to form OFPRA's "Eurafrica section" (sections are organized according asylum seekers' region of origin). In 2001 and 2002 the establishment of a new management team within the DAF signalled the beginning of OFPRA's gradual strengthening of the asylum bureaucracy at the border. OFPRA was within the Interior Ministry, but the DAF was attached to the Ministry of Foreign Affairs. The DAF now began to develop its own approach to asylum based on the context and objectives of border control, as well as the personality, management methods and vision of its leadership. Restrictive interpretations of asylum led to significant pressure to reduce admission. Rates of around 40 percent in 2001 fell to just under 20 percent in 2002, and dropped dramatically to 3.8 percent in 2003. At that point even OFPRA expressed disapproval of asylum examinations at the borders.

---

7 Minutes of the meeting between Anafé and OFPRA on the concept of "manifestly unfounded", 23 May 2007: http://www.anafe.org/download/generalites/CR%20r%E9union%20annuelle-version-assoc-16-04-07.pdf [accessed on 20 October 2018].

8 In 1991, 500 asylum claims were registered at the border. This figure increased to 4,409 in 2008, but decreased again to 1,180 in 2017, according to OFPRA annual reports (https://www.ofpra.gouv.fr/fr/l-ofpra/nos-publications/rapports-d-activite [accessed 20 October 2018].

9 Interview with M. Souza, a lawyer and member of the Anafé executive board, 18 March 2005 (all names have been anonymized).

The DAF hired fifteen new staff members in 2002 to replace the former team and respond to increased asylum requests. This new team was composed of young graduates with master's degrees hired on short term contracts. The job profile for protection officers did not call for specific legal knowledge: officers learned the ropes by observing their supervisors on the job, as one recalls:

> My first chief was Mr. L.: he was from the DGSE [Directorate General of Foreign Security, Foreign Intelligence Services of France] and had been a former spy. How should I put it... he was more a man of the action than a man of reflection. For him, 98 percent of asylum seekers were liars. My training was to watch my chief do the job. The first time I had a conversation with Mr. L., I was embarrassed because I felt that the criteria for judgment were absurd. I recall how, in an interview, he asked an asylum seeker to describe his cell and tell him how many square meters it was. The asylum seeker, anxious, responded "four square meters". At the end of the interview, M. L. told me: "You see, he's telling lies. There are no prison cells of four square meters!"
> (Interview with Élodie Noir, protection officer (OP) in the Border Asylum Division, 19 May 2005)

The youth and inexperience of this second team of DAF officers, their status on short term contracts, the lack of prerequisite skills, and the on-the-job training methods combined to diminish their autonomy and room for manoeuvre in 2002. This trend strengthened the tendency of the DAF to operate autonomously of refugee protection procedures as they were applied on French territory proper. However, on 21 July 2004, a new decree placed the DAF under OFPRA's supervision, where it remains today. In 2004, the asylum admission rate was 7.7 percent. Since 2005, the DAF's management has changed, but the daily routine of asylum examinations has remained the same since airport waiting zones opened in the early 1990s:

> In the morning there are envelopes with cases: we divide the interviews. At present there are only one or two [cases] per person per day, which is not much. The narratives are taken in their entirety and sent with notes to the chief, who has already received the report on the individual's situation by fax. [...] The chief either accepts our opinion or does not: he intervenes only to turn an agreement into a refusal. Then he sends his opinion to the DLPAJ [police]

who transfer it to the CASAI [Interior Ministry], which gives the final decision. The officers who issued opinions on "manifestly unfounded" claims no longer have any influence decisions from the moment the case is reviewed by the chief. (Interview with Élodie Noir, protection officer (OP) in the Border Asylum Division, 19 May 2005)

All asylum applications rejected at the border are called "manifestly unfounded". This is because refusal decisions at first screening rest on a country's legal right to reject "manifestly unfounded" applications that are false or fall outside the asylum framework. Refusal decisions are issued by the Directorate of Civil Liberties and Legal Affairs (DLPAJ) of the Interior Ministry, on official forms faxed from its offices in Paris. The notice most often comes on two sheets. The first part cites the legal texts governing the right to asylum in France, the asylum seeker's identity as officially registered (e.g. "Youssef Betrik alias Ali al-Darwi, born on 27/03/1980, declaring himself a Palestinian citizen") and the application date. The second part summarizes the asylum seeker's narrative in a few lines before stating, in a second paragraph, the OFPRA's reasons for refusal. The last part presents the DLPAJ's formal decision: the application is rejected, the applicant will be deported, the border police are "responsible for the notification and enforcement of this decision".

The asylum framework

On the morning of November 5, 2007, the Roissy police arrest Ahmed Masri while checking a flight from Hanoi, Vietnam. Ahmed asks for asylum at the police station and is transferred to the detention centre. There an OFPRA officer, a man in his thirties wearing a suit and a tie, hears the case in the late afternoon. The room, unlike others in the centre, has windows that can be opened, which overlook shrubs bordering the entrance way. In Arabic, the agent asks Ahmed to sit on the other side of the desk. The agent stands behind a computer and says to Ahmed: "I'm listening." As Ahmed speaks during the 20-minute interview, the agent takes notes on his computer. When Ahmed finishes speaking, he is asked if he has anything to add. Then he is asked to name the Jewish settlements close to his home. Afterwards, the OFPRA officer thanks him and takes him to the door. Ahmed takes his police papers and re-enters the hall, accompanied by one of the police officers at the desk. When they arrive on the first floor, the door of the refectory opens. Detainees are seated for the evening meal as the policeman brings Ahmed to join them.

At 1:30 am, Ahmed is in bed when a Red Cross employee comes to wake him up and asks him to go downstairs with his police papers. Ahmed rings the intercom in the hall, the door opens, and a policeman makes him enter and sit on one of the chairs along the corridor overlooking the police station. Then he comes back with a pile of papers. Ahmed signs two of them. One document extends his 48-hour stay in the waiting zone for another 48-hours. The other is a "notification of non-admission to asylum". He receives all the documents, which will be explained to him by the duty guard in the Red Cross office, where, evidently, insomniacs dwell. His rejection decision from the Interior Ministry reads:

> Considering that X [...], going by the name of Ahmed Masri, declares that he was born at Toulkarem and resided at Irtah; that he is of Palestinian origin; that he has no political activity or commitment; that he has not been threatened; that the land belonging to his family was confiscated by the Israeli army; that he had no professional activity; that life in the West Bank was difficult; that he would like to live in safety, in France, where he could work and provide for himself;
>
> Considering, however, that the applicant confines himself to invoking the economic situation which he would have experienced in Palestine; that there are no serious, direct and personal threats to him of any kind; whereas, moreover, he does not provide credible explanations concerning the exact conditions of his departure from Palestine; that he is ignorant of the area he claims to come from; that all his considerations are of an essentially economic nature and are connected with purely personal reasons, namely to find a job in France; therefore, his application does not meet the criteria laid down by the legislation governing asylum;
>
> Considering that he comes from Vietnam; Article L.213-4 of the Code on Entry and Residence of Foreigners and the Right of Asylum, prescribes his return to the territory of that State or, as the case may be, to any country where he will be legally eligible;

IT HAS BEEN DECIDED THAT:

Article 1: The application for entry into France in respect of the asylum of X alias Mr. MASRI is rejected.

Article 2: X alias Mr. MASRI will be redirected to the territory of Vietnam or, where applicable, to any country where he will be legally admissible.

Article 3: The police services at the borders shall be responsible for the notification and execution of this decision, a duplicate of which shall be given to the person concerned.

The next day, November 7, two days after his detainment in Roissy airport, Ahmed Masri goes to Anafé, the legal aid NGO working at the centre, to get more information. Kadra Benbedrik, a NGO worker, translates the decision into Arabic, then asks him to tell his story. Several times she asks if he personally fears anything in particular if he returns to Palestine. Each time, Ahmed answers by describing his living conditions in Irtah. Kadra concludes that she cannot make an appeal in favour of Ahmed: "the narrative is weak", "his case does not fit in the asylum framework," she notes on the day's balance sheet. However, she takes Ahmed's police papers and writes a letter to the Immigration Analysis and Monitoring Group (GASAI), asking if Ahmed could be sent to Jordan instead of back to Hanoi, where he spent only a few hours. Ahmed explains that he will certainly be detained for some time in Aman, which happens to all who try to migrate irregularly, but he prefers detention in Aman to returning to Vietnam. Later that evening, Ahmed is handcuffed and escorted to the airport for return to Hanoi. He struggles hard against being put on the plane. Finally, deportation does not take place, Ahmed is beaten by the police and spends another night in detention. In the days that follow, he resists four more attempts to return him to Hanoi.[10] On 14 November, he goes back to the Anafé office to speak again with Kadra. She accompanies him to the Red Cross office. Perhaps a mediator could speak with the police and try to negotiate Ahmed's deportation to Jordan (except she knows very well that this never happens). Two days later, Ahmed's name

---

10 The various practices associated with forced air deportation are detailed and analysed in Makaremi 2009.

no longer appears on the detention centre register. The Red Cross agent says they don't know what became of him. I also lose track of him.

In the waiting zone, the high stakes of selection, control and administration in treating asylum seekers are organized around distinctions between truth and falsehood. Here, I would like to reflect on how the practice of determining truth is constructed. In preparing this material, I do not have access to the interviews themselves, but only to re-transcriptions and syntheses by agents. Whereas the CNDA (the Appeals Court) is open to the public, and minutes of OFPRA agents' interviews on French soil are communicated to applicants when their applications are refused, in the waiting zone, the work of agents who listen to and transcribe narratives remains a blind spot for observers. It would be ideal to analyse the actual exchanges themselves, as they more clearly disclose standards of judgment. As an officer admits, these interactions insinuate mechanisms for discriminating against and rejecting asylum seekers within a procedure guaranteeing respect for asylum.

> I am asked to judge according to criteria that are not those of real life: I live in a universe with its criteria of judgments, but they no longer apply at all to the waiting area. [...] For example, at a party recently, I met a friend of a friend who was put in prison for two months in Tunisia where he was on vacation (he was mistaken for a trafficker) and he admitted that it was only two years later that he could talk about this experience. It is true that it is difficult to talk about something that has traumatized us.
> [...] There is also a difference between the objective threat as it is judged, and the fear that forces people to leave. [...] Yes, there is some schizophrenia and hypocrisy. Take the smugglers for instance: it is well known that sometimes asylum seekers cannot tell everything and hide with an awkward lie an episode as a smuggler. This used to be taken into account. But now the instruction is to use it as a pretext for refusal. (Interview with Elodie Noir, May 19, 2005)

The first distinction made in examining an asylum claim is between the application's form and its substance. In principle, the claimant's narrative recounts a situation corresponding to a sequence of events (including a threat and an escape), or describes his or her living conditions. The two axes of verification around which judgment is constructed are: "Is the narration true?" And "Does it place the subject in need of protection?" Processing applications shows that these two issues at stake – i.e. veracity and bodily peril – are inextricably linked in the framework of adjudication, as Ahmed Masri's case illustrates. We can thus identify categories that inform the French definition of asylum. Without entering, for the moment, into judgments of narrative truth and applicant credibility, we recognize four exclusionary arguments that delimit the framework of asylum in France – which will be discussed in turn in the subsequent sections. In the administrative jargon of the border administration, they make a refugee's claim *"manifestly unfounded"* as interpreted under the Geneva Convention.

The national definition of asylum is elaborated in decisions by OFPRA and the CNDA, but its chief manifestation in terms of jurisprudence comes from the French Supreme Court (*Conseil d'Etat*), the highest national court of appeal for refugee determination procedures. Supreme Court jurisprudence addresses both the substance of refugees' asylum requests (for instance, the decision that the threat of female genital mutilation falls within the scope of refugee protection) and the form (for instance, the decision favouring the admissibility of a particular document as supporting evidence for asylum applications). Jérôme Valluy (2009) has studied the uses and challenges of jurisprudential asylum definitions. In my work, some asylum definitions drawn by the border administration incorporate elements of jurisprudential definitions, but others are more vague or differ from national jurisprudence. Rather than comparing categories of definitions over time, my empirical perspective evaluates definitions and categorizations observed within a specific bureaucracy at a given time and place, and their relation to specific aims of the border apparatus.

"Manifestly unfounded"

The first criterion, the state criterion, recalls how the treatment of refugees is linked to a temporary suspension of state protection (Arendt 2002 [1951]). At first, the border administration conceived of protection only against threats emanating from state authorities. Since the 1990s, however, the definition of asylum has adapted to the changing reality of conflicts. In particular, analyses in international relations of "weak" states, "collapsed" states, and the privatization of conflicts (Rotberg 2003, Rotberg, Dadmehr and Jenne 2003) have resulted in a re-evaluation to account for threats emanating from private actors. However, OFPRA agents view this source of threat with great suspicion, and subject it to criteria that maintain state hegemony in ideas defining conflict and protection. Indeed, each asylum seeker must show evidence that the state did not or could not afford him necessary protection.

> He states that he did not seek protection from the Nigerian authorities, even though the said authorities would have been able to provide him with effective protection.

This criterion – lack of State protection – is not universal. It is not necessary in the Canadian asylum system, for example, where 70 percent of asylum requests are accepted (USCRI 2008). Yet it is just one reason why asylum refusals are much higher in France. Other factors are the link between asylum and immigration, asylum being increasingly considered as another immigration route in Europe and in North America, and differences in French and Canadian national cultures when facing the phenomenon of migration. For instance, Colombians who are able to go into exile and seek asylum abroad are generally well-off, with resources that make them desirable to the Canadian government. By contrast, France, with a European conception of "zero immigration", seems to establish criteria that exclude as many asylum applicants from the judicial process as possible, without attaching any particular importance to the socio-cultural situation or the potential "contribution" of different refugee groups.

A second criterion– the "general situation of insecurity" – is related to the first exclusion criterion. It is interesting to note that this criterion distinguishes the French definition of asylum from definitions in jurisdictions whose legal tradition is derived from English common law.

> She does not allege any personal threat to her; she merely refers to the general situation of insecurity prevailing in Haiti.

Indeed, in the specific reading developed by the DAF, following OFPRA, asylum applications due to situations of structural insecurity are *a priori* refused, except where a request presents an additional element of individual threat. Thus, among the asylum applications that I had the opportunity to see in the field (beyond the forty-eight cases studied here), descriptions of living condition without personal narratives of dangerous events are systematically classified as outside the purview of asylum procedure. This definition of vulnerability and protection is at odds with practices in Canadian, American, Australian and British jurisdictions, which include general insecurity as a fundamental criterion in determining the need for protection. Conversely in France, an individual conception of asylum prevails. Applicants whose daily living conditions justify the need for protection are excluded on the grounds that their applications do not correspond to an individual trajectory, but to a collective projection. The discourse of asylum rejection is generally based on the figure of the false refugee, an economic migrant who invents false needs for protection. Whereas situations of "generalized insecurity" are recognized as living situations that require protection, belonging to a group that is subject to threats is disqualifying if no personal narrative distinguishes an applicant's singular situation from that of his or her fellow citizens (as in the case of Ahmed Masri).

Indeed, the "general situation of insecurity" is one of four official criteria named by the DAF's director as important in substantiating assessments of "manifestly unfounded" claims.[11] However, asylum applications from certain nationalities are largely accepted in practice: according to figures released by the Ministry of the Interior, 83 percent of Iraqi asylum-seekers and 63 percent of Sri Lankan asylum-seekers were admitted in 2007, while 30 percent of all asylum applications filed at the border were accepted (Anafé 2008).

A third exclusion criterion – "the absence of personal threats" – echoes "generalized insecurity" by highlighting the individual concept of protection defended by French asylum doctrine. Fear of persecution, the basis of the Geneva Convention's definition of refugee, is defined in French doctrine as the presence of clearly identifiable and attestable personal threats.

> He is not able to explain to what extent he would be threatened in case of return to the Congo.
> He does not mention any direct and personal threat to him from anybody.

Behind this perception of the refugee is the idea that the applicant bears individual responsibility for the persecution victimizing him or her. France offers protection to individual refugees involved in political activity, as con-

---

11 Minutes of the meeting between Anafé and the OFPRA on the concept of "manifestly unfounded", *Ibid*.

firmed by the experience of Abdoulaye Ita. After his brother fled Chad to come to France, where he was given refugee status, Chadian authorities sought Abdoulaye Ita, suspecting him of knowing where his brother had taken refuge. Abdoulaye was refused asylum in August 2004 after meeting with OFPRA, however, because "he was not involved in any political activity".

In this frame of analysis, a final exclusion criterion – the "motive of pure personal convenience" – places applicants outside the field of asylum. Confirming a definition of asylum aligned with representations of political refugees (Noiriel 1991), the notion of "personal convenience" refers to personal elements, such as health, illness or family situations, that break the linear confrontation between the applicant and the power that threatens and targets him or her. As events necessitating escape become more distant in time, the asylum narrative is increasingly undermined and touched by the intrusion of personal considerations outside the tragic framework (the naked scene of oppression and resistance). Narratives are ultimately disqualified by such intrusions. Known as "pure personal conveniences", the necessary but unwelcome dimensions of life (such as family ties, psychic comfort, health status) disrupt and parasitize political tragedies that legitimize the use of asylum in the context of migration control. As an administrative judge told two Congolese children, a brother and sister who were juvenile asylum-seekers:

> You're talking about an indirect threat, because your father is concerned. The only thing that is established, without any proof, is the death of Mademoiselle's mother. And again, the soldiers did not come specially to kill her; she took a bullet as she went out. [...] I understand that this is not an easy situation, but the asylum procedure must be strictly reserved for people who have no other solutions. You know what is happening in most African countries, one could tell the same kind of narrative that you did.[12]

This kind of judgement, which makes it possible to exclude all requests that fall "outside the field" of asylum, is only one dimension of asylum adjudication. It relates to the substance of the narrative and seeks to ascertain whether the claim is genuine. Another, more important issue is whether the claim is true. This issue is linked to the form of the narrative. However, these

---

12 Field notes, Administrative Court, 5 April 2007.

two factors are closely aligned as motives for refusal decisions, which pass fluidly from one argument to the other.

The truth of the narrative: the technical sense and the moral sense of truth

How do we approach the process of truth determination at work in judging the applicant's narrative and spoken performance? Bernard Williams' genealogical study of truth determination (Williams 2002) is an interesting starting point for investigating adjudication processes that lead to an assessment of claims as "manifestly unfounded". Williams seeks to identify the intellectual and moral approaches, both scientific and casual, that guide our judgment of the veracity of a proposition – of its truth. For Williams, distinguishing truth from falsehood relies upon two "virtues of truth": sincerity opposes truth to lies, and accuracy opposes truth to error. These categories appear in the judgments of Border Asylum Division agents. DAF agents evaluate sincerity based on the applicant's subjective and emotional involvement in his or her narrative ("conventional", "impersonal", "stereotyped", "not very loquacious"), marked by the use of certain recurring narrative patterns (mentioning places of custody or means of escape). They also evaluate the criterion of likelihood ("the conditions are not credible", "unreliable"), simultaneously scrutinizing context and probability, and attributing intelligibility to the narrator's rational behaviour ("It is surprising that, having first crossed the French border to go to Dubai, she did not think of asking for asylum at that time").

This set of norms regulating the asylum narrative are culturally determined, referring to shared conceptions of what is "likely" or unlikely, or what makes speech "emotional" (Belorgey 2003, d'Halluin 2004, Crépeau et al 2001, Rousseau and Foxen 2006, Valluy 2009). Reaching a judgement here also implies an appreciation of accuracy, not this time in terms of assessing narrative norms, but rather in the application of norms of examination. Thus, the administration claims that its method determines the truth based on criteria of clarity ("confusing", "obscure"), accuracy ("the statements of the person's concerns are vague", "He is not in a position to say, even approximately, how many times he was placed in police custody") and verification ("without any conclusive explanation", "without detailed evidence", "the documents showed do not contain any guarantee of authenticity", "without bringing any tangible element in support of this information"). These judgements rest on the epistemic norms that underlie any empirical or logical statement, including this ethnographic work. The criterion of verification raises the question of producing evidence and certificates (Fassin and d'Halluin 2005, d'Halluin 2006b, Fassin and Rechtman 2007). The need to substantiate and empirically validate applicants' narratives implies an administrative logic of proofs. In an interview, an OFPRA agent expressed his aversion to this analysis. But he admitted that he finds verification issues at different levels:

> The request for written evidence is an extrapolation of the Anafé.[13] Concerning the case mentioned in the report of the association (Anafé 2004) [a former bodyguard of Laurent Kabila, whose application was rejected until he produced a picture showing him in the exercise of his duties as bodyguard, was mentioned as an example of OFPRA's onerous requirements for concrete evidence], this guy was auditioned by me and indeed I was sure he was telling lies. I was very surprised when he showed me the picture, I really thought he was lying [...] there are so many people who claim that they were Kabila's bodyguards!
> [...] Once I asked for information about a Rwandan asylum application: I did not know what to decide so I sent a note to a regional analyst of the Ministry of Foreign Affairs who contacted the Embassy of France on site. The Embassy of France replied that there were no problems, so no threats on the point in question. But we know they do not know everything. Later, the analyst told me: "I think it was a mistake". I did not know what to decide so I asked the advice of a third party. But I knew what the answer was going to be when I asked. When a case is difficult to judge, a third opinion from the Ministry of Foreign Affairs is sought, knowing that this opinion will always be on the side of refusal. (Interview with Julien Robert, Contractual Protection Officer (OP) at the Border Asylum Division, 3 July 2007)

---

13 The case mentioned in the association report was that of a former bodyguard of Laurent Kabila, whose asylum application had been rejected until he showed a photo of him performing his duties as a bodyguard. This example denounced the tendency of the asylum division to require documentary evidence to believe applicants' stories (Anafé 2004).

Verification criteria, both scientific and legal, reveal how truth determination mobilizes issues of method, resulting from rational determination, and of judgment, calling for "intimate conviction".

The criterion of accuracy slides towards a third stratum – the moral domain. Determinations of clarity and precision are apparent in refusal decisions: "he remains evasive", "she is totally incapable of giving the slightest detail", "he is elusive". Opinions drawn from rhetorical or semantic methods evoke moral connotations. Moral evaluations of applicants distinguish a set of postures that qualify the oral narrative: notions of deception and also of cooperation and good faith are particularly distinguished:

> He cannot clearly state the reasons for his departure while the protection officer repeatedly asked him to focus his statements on recent events. [He] dwells on facts from the 1990s, without giving the reasons for his departure from Turkey in 2007.
> He keeps asserting, laconically, that he was beaten, while remaining silent on interrogations.

These statements characterize different levels of verification in manifestly unfounded asylum narratives. I refer to Williams to understand two dimensions of the production of truth that appear in asylum examinations. One refers to assertion (produced by the applicant), and the other to belief (the "intimate conviction" at the core of the OFPRA agent's judgment). Williams distinguishes these two poles by recalling the relational dimension of the production of truth engaged in an "epistemic division of labor" (Williams 2002: 43) between the one who states and the one who receives and judges the statement's veracity. If sincerity is virtuous, conveying truth in the enunciation of a proposition or the narration of a fact, ascertaining veracity also implies virtue in commitment to apprehending and judging the truth, which Williams calls the "investigative investment" (Williams 2002: 124). On the one hand, the figure of the "refugee-liar" (Rousseau and Foxen 2006) is based on assessments of sincerity, which I tried to understand via the semantic categories used to qualify lies. On the other hand, the time OFPRA agents devote to interviews, the formal requirements, judgment stereotypes and superficial information about cultures and countries of origin, show meagre "investment" (Belorgey 2003, Belorgey 2007, Valluy 2009). The discursive system of the "manifestly unfounded" claim, with its codes, themes, and obligatory stages, rests on two fictions (Decourcelle 2002, Belorgey 2007): the agent's good faith, and the asylum seeker's capacity to summon biographical linearity and narrate his or her life clearly and concisely. The notion of "mistrust" used to describe the experience of the refugee (Daniel and Knudsen 1995) helps explain this space of suspicion where narrative is expressed or hidden.

In this game of utterance and conviction that determines truthfulness, Williams shows with pertinence that the truth at play is not of indivisible or unconditional value, and that it is not at stake in the same way for the one who states and the one who receives. At stake in sincerity is "should I tell the truth?" and "how much of the truth should I tell?" Thus, there is more or less truth. At stake in conviction is not the existence of truth ("must I believe in the truth?"). For receivers who admit that truth exists, the question then becomes, "Will I bother to find out about it?"

> There is this difference that in defining accuracy we must mention the truth, while with sincerity the reference to truth only comes to the next step. (Williams 2002: 126)

Analysing the values that define and underpin the question of truth in asylum examination shows how practices of administrative control and categorisation of asylum seekers are tied together in the moral and epistemological dimensions that shape the narrative of asylum.

Memory and the state

Certainly, the administrative world of border control is a microcosm, with logics of emancipation related to the supervisory administration of national territory. But the administrative machine also mirrors myths and national values forged in public spaces. Proposing an analysis that complements and critically addresses both the Frankfurt School's work on the modern episteme of administrative rationality (Adorno and Horkheimer 1997) and Hannah Arendt's observations on the banality of evil (Arendt 1965), Michael Herzfeld demonstrates how administrative categorization applies a national logic that seeks to "distinguish between those included and excluded from the national order and to represent these distinctions as given by nature –

rather than cultural or historical contingencies." (Herzfeld 1992: 174). Reflections on administrative rationality in the aftermath of the Second World War tended to see it as a self-referential mechanism capable of applying almost any national policy via unique systems of hierarchies and rationalities. Yet, Herzfeld guided his empirical investigations in a different direction. For him, the categorization practices underlying administrative rationality depend strongly on national circumstances, inasmuch as they are produced by national memory of who is included and who is excluded from national belonging: "The power to refuse Hospitality is the foundation on which indifference rests: it is a denial of the common substance." (Herzfeld 1992: 177). In this respect, it is significant that, after President Nicolas Sarkozy's election in 2007, the agencies referred to in this chapter were reorganized and merged into a single ministerial body called the Department of Immigration, Integration, *National Identity* and Solidarity Development.

The name of this new ministry permits the introduction of the idea that the process of asylum application and asylum itself are part of a broader set of relations between populations seeking asylum and administrations interpreting asylum in terms of post-colonial memories of power relations. In the novel, *Transit*, written by Djiboutian author Abdourahman A. Waberi, the protagonist, Harbi, an asylum seeker waiting at Roissy airport, bogs down in a bitter soliloquy:

> I cannot wait to find peace of mind and body again. To tame my mind where morbid, incongruous ideas keep running wild, and snuff out that snickering little voice. Glue the pieces of my dislocated being back together. In short, get used to my new identity. A memory anchored deep in the nest of my brain is coming back to me. I must have been a child of four or five then, and I can recall the frightened look in my eyes very clearly. One day, as I was walking with my aunt along one of the avenues in our neighborhood, I passed by a military patrol. Like a chrysalis about to burst, the question popped out instantly:
> "Who are those people?"
>
> "The French, our colonizers."

"Why are they here?"

"Because they're stronger than we are." (Waberi 2003: 17)

Here, free association of the narrator's thoughts links his memory of the colonial past with his present situation of confinement after his asylum request. Why does this memory resurface during the border transit? In the literary fiction Waberi imagines, Harbi's memory of colonial domination and its actualization in the contemporary global context contribute to configuring the practices of forced migration and asylum. This dimension stands out clearly in the administrative practice of granting more credit to certain asylum stories than to others based on country of origin. The French state has long applied a special kindness towards refugees from Rwanda that, it may be supposed, is related to France's ambiguous engagement in the Rwandan conflict and the failures of French intervention during these events (Prunier 1997). Another example of how political considerations connected to post-colonial memories and contemporary power relations shape the asylum system occurred in the winter of 2004-2005. Hundreds of Ivorian asylum seekers were rejected and sent back to Côte d'Ivoire in an acute climate of violence that presaged civil war. When the French army tried to intervene in the Ivorian conflict, its troops were attacked and denounced for conducting an operation of "post-colonial domination"; they eventually withdrew from the conflict (Marshall 2005). On Christmas night 2004, an Ivorian asylum seeker rejected by OFPRA cut his throat to resist deportation. A few days later, a Congolese asylum seeker from a refugee camp in Côte d'Ivoire, who had left during xenophobic attacks that had massacred part of the camp's refugee population, was rejected by OFPRA and sent back under escort to Côte d'Ivoire. A legal refugee in Côte d'Ivoire, Ernest Businga had brought with him several letters addressed to the UN High Commissioner for Refugees (UNHCR) in Geneva, requesting transfer to another country where he would be safe. These letters were authenticated by the UNHCR office in Paris, but the Ministry of the Interior held to its decision to reject and expel Ernest Businga, arguing that, although he was a statutory refugee who feared threats and had tried for months to seek the High Commissioner's protection from the violence to which he was exposed, his refugee status fell under the Convention of the Organization of African Unity (OAU) and not the Geneva Convention, to which France is a party. By taking the trouble to argue why it had abandoned Ernest Businga to his fate, the administration's position quite clearly echoed France's withdrawal from regional issues in West Africa. This highlights the political stakes that underpin the selection of those with rights to national protection and others caught in the ramifications of diplomatic affinities and tensions in the arena of asylum. Ernest was finally removed by force (*"bien embarqué"*). For a few months I continued to receive his emails: he was hidden, terrified, asking for help.

Conclusion

The administrative elision of individual narratives entails the conjunction of various factors. These heterogeneous elements all stem from perceptions by French authorities of the migration "problem" and the asylum administration that results from this perception, its disciplinary management of flows of asylum seekers and its fight against perceived abuses of the welfare system. Migration and the control of migration confine asylum seekers in processes of subjectivation articulated around issues of mis/trust. Exile narration is the basis for asylum procedure administration. Yet, such narration confronts bureaucratic rationalities anchored in national logics and memory. It defies demands for linearity in support of truthfulness and ethical judgment, which suspends confiscated and alternative narrations[14] – the confused work of a living memory:

> Something we might tentatively call the truth of the person, a truth that, to a certain degree [...] might well become more clear in moments of interruption, stoppage, open-endedness – in enigmatic articulations that cannot be translated into narrative form. (Butler 2005: 64)

As this chapter's observations show, I have not had access to this singular "truth", but to violent discrepancies that, at times, make one suspect its existence. In her definition of living memory, Judith Butler states, however, that her goal is not to celebrate

---

14 These dimensions, referring to the lived experiences of border detention, are analysed in Makaremi 2011.

a certain notion of incoherence, but only to point out that our "incoherence" establishes the way in which we are constituted in relationality: implicated, beholden, derived, sustained by a social world that is beyond us and before us. (Butler 2005: 65)

The ordinary violence of border detention resides partly in the collapse and illegibility of this social world. Defiance links migrants to the violence of interpellation (Althusser 1976, Butler 2005), where they are constituted as the subjects of a control. It links them through a violent imposition of silence, where the "incoherence" of singular narratives binds them in an implacable procedure that unfolds from a fissured relationality to the exercise of force.

Bibliography

Adorno, Theodor W., and Max Horkheimer. 1997. *Dialectic of Enlightenment*. London: Verso Books.

Akoka, Karen. 2019. La fabrique des réfugiés dans la Guerre froide: une ethnographie historique des 'vingt glorieuses' de l'attribution de l'asile en France (1952-1972). *Politique et Sociétés* 38(1): 19–48.

Anafé. 2004. *La frontière et le droit: la zone d'attente de Roissy sous le regard de l'Anafé. Bilan de six mois d'observation associative (avril-octobre 2004).*: http://www.anafe.org/download/rapports/Anaf%E9 Bilan nov 04.pdf [accessed 29 October 2009].

Anafé. 2008. *Statistiques relatives aux étrangers à la frontière. Novembre 2008*: http://www.anafe.org/download/generalites/stats-za-nov2008.pdf [accessed 2 August 2009].

Anafé. 2016. "Des zones d'atteintes aux droits". *Rapport d'observations dans les zones d'attente et Rapport d'activité*, Novembre 2015. Paris: Anafé.

Arendt, Hannah. 1965. *Eichmann in Jerusalem: a Report on the Banality of Evil*. Rev. and enl. ed. New York: Viking Press.

Arendt, Hannah. 1982 [1951]. *Les origines du totalitarisme vol. 2. L'impérialisme*. Paris: Fayard.

Belorgey, Jean-Marie. 2003. "Le contentieux du droit d'asile et l'intime conviction du juge. *Revue Administrative* (336): 619–622.

Belorgey, J.-M. 2007. Le droit d'asile en perdition. *TERRA-Ed., Coll. "Reflets"* (mai 2007): http://terra.rezo.net/article598.html [accessed 29 October 2009].
Butler, Judith. 2005. *Giving an Account of Oneself.* New York: Fordham University Press.
Crépeau, François. 1995. *Droit d'asile: de l'hospitalité aux contrôles migratoires.* Bruxelles: Éditions Bruylant.
Crépeau, F., P. Foxen, F. Houle, and C. Rousseau. 2001. Analyse multidisciplinaire du processus décisionnel de la CISR. *Refuge* 19 (4): 62–75.
d'Halluin, Estelle. 2004. Comment produire un discours légitime ? *Plein Droit* (63): 30–33.
Daniel, E. Valentine, and John C. Knudsen. 1995. *Mistrusting Refugees.* Berkeley: University of California Press.
Decourcelle, Antoine. 2002. Asile: administration de la preuve. *Vacarme* (18): http://www.vacarme.org/article232.html [accessed 29 October 2009].
Fassin, Didier. 2001b. Quand le corps fait loi. La raison humanitaire dans les procédures de régularisation des étrangers. *Sciences sociales et santé* 19 (4): 5–42.
Fassin, Didier., and E. d'Halluin. 2005. The Truth from the Body: Medical Certificates as Ultimate Evidence for Asylum Seekers. *American Anthropologist* 107 (4): 597–608.
Fassin, Didier and Richard Rechtman. 2007. *L'Empire du traumatisme. Enquête sur la condition de victime.* Paris: Flammarion.
Fassin, Didier. 2013. The Precarious Truth of Asylum. *Public Culture* 25 (1 (69)): 39–63.
Fassin, Didier, and Carolina Kobelinsky. 2012. Comment on juge l'asile. *Revue française de sociologie* 53 (4): 657–688.
Foucault, Michel. 2004a. *Naissance de la biopolitique: cours au Collège de France (1978–1979), Hautes études.* Paris: Gallimard/Seuil.
Foucault, Michel. 2004b. *Sécurité, territoire, population: cours au Collège de France (1977–1978), Hautes études.* Paris: Seuil/Gallimard.
Herlihy, Jane, Kate Gleeson, and Stuart Turner. 2010. What Assumptions About Human Behaviour Underlie Asylum Judgements? *International Journal of Refugee Law* 22. (3): 351–366.
Herzfeld, Michael. 1992. *The Social Production of Indifference: Exploring the Symbolic Roots of Western Bureaucracy, Global Issues.* New York: Berg.

Kobelinsky, Carolina. 2012. L'asile gay: jurisprudence de l'intime à la Cour nationale du droit d'asile. *Droit et société* (3): 583–601.

Kobelinsky, Carolina. 2015. Judging Intimacies at the French Court of Asylum. *PoLAR: Political and Legal Anthropology Review* 38(3): 338–355.

Kynsilehto, Anitta, and Eeva Puumala. 2015. Persecution as Experience and Knowledge: the Ontological Dynamics of Asylum Interviews. *International Studies Perspectives* 16 (4): 446–462.

Lavenex, Sandra. 1999. *The Europeanisation of Refugee Policies: Between Human Rights and Internal Security*. Aldershot: Ashgate.

Makaremi, Chowra. 2008. Etudier et assister les étrangers aux frontières. In Didier Fassin and Alban Bensa, eds, *Les politiques de l'enquête: épreuves ethnographiques*. Paris: La Découverte.

Makaremi, Chowra. 2009a. Governing Borders in France: From Extraterritorial to Humanitarian Confinement. *Canadian Journal of Law and Society* 24 (3): 411–432.

Makaremi, Chowra. 2009b. Violence et refoulement dans la zone d'attente de Roissy. In Carolina Kobelinsky and Chowra Makaremi, eds, *Enfermés dehors. Enquête sur le confinement des étrangers*. Bellecombes-en-Beauge: Editions du Croquant: 41–62

Makaremi, Chowra. 2011. The Waiting Zone. In Julia Creet and Andreas Kitzmann, eds, *Memory and Migration: Multidisciplinary Approaches to Memory Studies*. University of Toronto Press.

Marrus, Marc. R. 1985. *The Unwanted: European Refugees in the Twentieth Century*. New York: Oxford University Press.

Marshall, Robert. 2005. La France en Côte d'Ivoire: L'interventionnisme à l'épreuve des faits. *Politique africaine* 98: 21–41.

Maskens, Maïté. 2015. Bordering Intimacy: The Fight Against Marriages of Convenience in Brussels. *The Cambridge Journal of Anthropology* 33 (2): 42–58.

Noiriel, Gérard. 1991. *La tyrannie du national: le droit d'asile en Europe, 1793-1993, Histoire, les temps qui courent*. Paris: Calmann-Lévy.

Noiriel, Gérard. 1992. *Population, immigration et identité nationale en France: XIXe-XXe siècle, Carré Histoire ; 17*. Paris: Hachette.

OFPRA. 2016. *Office français de protection des réfugiés et apatrides: Rapport d'activité 2008*: http://www.ofpra.gouv.fr/.../Rapport_Ofpra_2008_complet_BD.pdf [accessed 28 October 2015].

Palluel, Christelle. 2016. Le nouveau régime de la demande d'asile en rétention administrative: des garanties en trompe-l'œil, *La Revue des droits de l'homme* 10.

Prunier, Georges. 1997. *The Rwanda Crisis: History of a Genocide*. New York: Columbia University Press.

Ricœur, Paul. 1965. *De l'interprétation*. Paris: Seuil.

Rotberg, Robert I. 2003a. *When States Fail: Causes and Consequences*. Princeton, NJ: Princeton University Press.

Rotberg, Robert I., Nasrin Dadmehr, and Erin Jenne. 2003b. *State Failure and State Weakness in a Time of Terror*. Washington, DC: Brookings Institution Press.

Rousseau, Cécile., and Patricia Foxen. 2006. Le mythe du réfugié menteur: un mensonge indispensable? *Evolution psychiatrique* 71 (3): 505–520.

Schuster, Lisa. 2005. *The Realities of a New Asylum Paradigm*. Oxford: Centre on Migration, Policy & Society.

Simich, Laura. 2003. Negotiating Boundaries of Refugee Resettlement: A Study of Settlement Patterns and Social Support. *The Canadian Review of Sociology and Anthropology* 40 (5): 575–592.

Sirkeci, Ian. 2005. War in Iraq: Environment of Insecurity and International Migration. *International Migration* 43 (4): 197–214.

USCRI. 2015. US Committee for Refugees and Immigrants. *World Refugee Survey 2008 – Canada* (19 June 2008): http://www.unhcr.org/refworld/docid/485f50c776.html (29/10/2016).

Valluy, Jerome. 2009. *Rejet des exilés: le grand retournement du droit d'asile*. Bellecombe-en-Beauges: Editions du Croquant.

Waberi, Abdourahman A. 2003. *Transit*. Paris: Gallimard.

Williams, Bernard. 2002. *Truth & Truthfulness: an Essay in Genealogy*. Princeton, NJ: Princeton University Press.

Moral Economy and Knowledge Production in a Security Bureaucracy
The Case of the German Office for the Protection of the Constitution

Werner Schiffauer

Germany's 1999/2000 citizenship law marked a shift in the country's self-definition from a non-immigration country to an immigration country. The general opening up of the German nation-state was soon followed by new closures, however. Discussions began on who should, and who should not be accepted as members of the re-invented nation-state. The debate centred on Muslim immigrants. How can Muslim immigrants become part of Germany when they adhere to a religion (and culture) with a long historical position as the quintessential other to European culture and society? What place, in particular, should be assigned to Muslim organisations that provide for doctrine and ritual? As the new Islamic presence in Germany was considered a key challenge for maintaining public security and order, the Ministry of the Interior took the lead in policy development. Within the ministry, security agencies, particularly the Office for the Protection of the Constitution (*Verfassungsschutz*) played a decisive role in generating knowledge about the newcomers and the structure and formation of Islamic politics.

In this paper, I analyse the ways in which security knowledge is produced in the Ämter für Verfassungsschutz, the "Offices for the Protection of the Constitution".[1] I apply an emic approach, asking how bureaucrats in this institution perceive and categorise Islam, to show how this knowledge constitutes the foundation for various security strategies. I begin by sketching the mission and the vision of the *Verfassungsschutz* and exploring how ideas

---

1 The offices for the Protection of the Constitution consist of one Federal Office (*Bundesamt*), part of the Federal Ministry of the Interior, and 16 state offices (*Länderämter*).

about the work ethos and work ethics of office holders are derived from the tasks assigned to them. By analysing one specific product of the work of the *Verfassungsschutz* (a PowerPoint presentation), I show how its vision and mission are translated into a classificatory system characterised by impervious grids. The structural properties of this knowledge, as well as its limitations, are made visible by contrasting it to knowledge obtained by participant observation. Seen in this light, *Verfassungsschutz* classifications appear as categorical straightjackets that fail to capture the dynamics and complexities of Islamic and Islamist communities. This failure, however, remains largely unnoticed in the bureaucratic apparatus, as security knowledge and security practices – such as surveillance and discipline – are intertwined. Conflicts with other state agencies favouring more biopolitical or pedagogical approaches (my example is the field of "de-radicalisation" politics) and moves in favour of more qualitative approaches occasionally emerge, but most are "resolved" in favour of classical security knowledge.

The background to this paper was my constant irritation with the German state's view of Islamic communities as I carried out anthropological field research on the Cologne-based organisation self-described as *Kalifatstaat* ("Caliphate State") between 1990 and 2000 and on the Muslim community Millî Görüş between 2000 and 2010 (Schiffauer 2000; 2010). I was confronted with the fact that state agencies systematically interpreted identical observations differently than I did. This experience was the beginning of this research project aimed at an emic understanding of knowledge production in the security agencies. Since the security establishment proved to be largely inaccessible, direct participant observation was only possible for Islamic actors.

Ethos and ethics in bureaucracies

Ethics are a good point of departure if one wants to understand bureaucracies from an emic perspective. A focus on ethics means asking how moral ideas shape the work of civil servants. This allows access to the self-understanding of professional civil servants and provides an answer to the question: "What do they think they are doing?" (Eckert in this volume), and also: "What do they think they should be doing?"[2]

These questions are related to the vision and the mission of a bureaucracy, which specifies the services a bureaucracy owes society and clarifies the value society obtains from these particular services. Vision and mission are usually formulated by reference to the common good of the nation-state. The mandate of the office defines the ways in which it serves the common good, whether by collecting taxes,[3] organising school infrastructure, engaging in urban planning or providing security. The status of a bureaucracy, as reflected in its annual budget allocations, depends upon the answers to these questions.

The ethics of a specific bureaucracy are derived from these mission statements. They serve as a yardstick that distinguishes good from bad bureaucratic work. The former fulfils the mandate of the office and adds to its value; the latter does not. The ideal thus formulated is never realised completely, but an institution may not depart from it too much – otherwise it is called to order. The vision and the mission of an office are celebrated and regularly remembered at ceremonial events such as political receptions or the appointment of new directors.

Julia Eckert (in this volume) introduces a distinction between ethics and ethos. While the ethics of an office refers to its substantive goals, its ethos refers to its standards of implementation. The work has to be carried out in a way that corresponds to bureaucratic reason. The rationality proclaimed by all state bureaucracies is coherence and consistency; as well as regularity and calculability. Equal cases should be treated the same. This implies an idea of serving the public in an accountable, unbiased, verifiable and controlled, but also in efficient and reliable, way. Like ethics, the ethos of an office is specified by its mandate.

It should be mentioned here that state bureaucracies follow different ethics. Following Foucault's distinction of different types of governmentalities (Foucault 2006a), one can make a key distinction between bureaucracies practicing governmentalities of discipline and surveillance, and bureaucracies practic-

---

[2] The case of the *Verfassungsschutzämter* is a particular case in point. The value of information provided by them was seriously called in question after the end of the Cold War in 1989. There were debates about abolishing them altogether. The Islamist challenge after September 11 enabled the agency to prove its usefulness in the post-Cold War period.

[3] See David Foster Wallace's enlightening discussion of the ethos and ethics of a tax bureaucracy (Wallace 2011).

ing "bio-political" governmentalities. The former see their task as maintaining security and order; the latter find their raison d'être in enabling positive developments, and emphasise control and regulation. This difference is reflected in their respective ethics. Ministries of the interior abide by strikingly different ethics from ministries of family and social affairs or ministries of education. The analysis of ethics allows us to overcome one serious problem of studies of the state: too often the unity of the state is overemphasised, and existing differences between bureaucracies are underestimated. Analysis of the different ethics allows us to conceive of the state as an arena of contestation over how to serve the public good meaningfully and effectively. Additionally, there can be contradictions between ethics and ethos, as Eckert has pointed out. Formally correct actions that are dictated by the work ethos can impede accomplishment of tasks demanded by the ethics of the office. Police officers complaining that legal prescriptions hinder them in carrying out their work in an efficient way are a good example. In these instances, conflicts regularly arise between those in the office demanding exceptions in order to cope with the challenges at hand (and thus do justice to the ethics of the office) and those who defend the ethos of orderly and consistent procedure that guarantees equal treatment of equal cases. While the former consider the latter to be inflexible and stubborn, the latter see the former as acting in an arbitrary fashion. Again, the terminology of ethics and ethos allows us to conceptualise a given bureaucracy as a field of contestation where tension between ethics and ethos is negotiated.

Ethos and ethics in the Offices for the Protection of the Constitution

The Offices for the Protection of the Constitution (*Verfassungsschutzämter*) are domestic intelligence agencies. Their task is to obtain knowledge of planned anti-constitutional activities at an early stage and provide this information to public authorities and (to a limited extent) the general public. The laws that regulate the duties of the *Verfassungsschutzämter* draw two ethical lessons from the traumas of German history. On the one hand, a lesson is drawn from the failure of the Weimar Republic. According to the dominant narrative of history, the democratic centre was crushed by mutually reinforcing radicalism on both left and right, culminating in the National Socialist takeover. Unlike the Weimar Republic, which gave too much space to the enemies of democracy, the Federal Republic is supposed to be a *wehrhafte Demokratie*, a "militant democracy" capable of actively defending its democratic substance.[4] The *Verfassungsschutzämter* consider themselves to be the institutional embodiment of this idea. But a lesson may be drawn from the second trauma, which is National Socialism itself. The *Verfassungsschutzämter* must never become a second secret state police (Gestapo). It should be powerful, but must not be in a position to abuse this power. This obvious dilemma is met, above all, by separating intelligence and police action. The *Verfassungsschutzämter* observe and produce knowledge, but refrain from taking action themselves. They have the power of definition, but not of coercion. As an "early warning system", they inform political authorities, other government agencies and the general public about their findings and enable them to take appropriate steps.[5] The connection between state knowledge production and state action is interrupted and an interface is installed, which should allow control of the office. In sum, the ethics of the *Verfassungsschutzämter* are derived from their self-understanding as intelligence agencies in the service of democracy and the rule of law, which is specified by the lessons drawn from the experience of Germany history.

Two further specifications resulting from this self-understanding deserve special mention. The first emphasises early or timely information. The idea is to produce knowledge about *potential* dangers: protecting the constitution requires not only observing groups whose danger is proven, but also those that could be dangerous in the future (ibid.). This ensures the effectiveness of the office. State and society must be informed about developments when they are still in a position to take effective measures. The second is an obligation that the information gathered be made public. This is put into practice through the publication of annual reports, and via exhibitions and special events. The agency must justify why certain groups appear in their reports. Disclosure implies accountability.

This knowledge production is now subject to a special ethos. Several aspects deserve to be mentioned in this context. In order to control the power of the *Verfassungsschutz*, the acquisition of information is subject to strong limitations. The *Verfassungsschützer* are not allowed to carry out inter-

---

4 This narrative structures the presentation of the history of the Federal Republic in schoolbooks (see, Baumann et. al 2002: 33ff).
5 Gesetz über den Verfassungsschutz in Berlin §5 (1).

rogations (this is reserved for the police) or to conduct surveys. The office relies mostly on written analyses and informants. Other aspects of their ethos relate to the general observance of neutrality and impartiality characteristic of all public authorities. The demand is that different extremisms be treated analogously, that is, they should not be blind in the "right" eye, the "left" eye or the "Islamic" eye. Finally, the offices have developed a distinctive set of rules aimed at guaranteeing objectivity. Direct contact between evaluators and persons who are being monitored is forbidden in order to prevent identification and "going native". Field data can only be collected indirectly through informants. The co-operation of evaluators, providers and informants has been aptly described by Yassin Musharbash:

> [...] the employees are divided into two tribes: "providers" spend a lot of time outside the offices. They recruit and lead informants – these are mostly shady figures from extremist milieus, who sell information to the service[...] Their insider knowledge [...] sometimes also leads to arrests, the banning of an organisation or the thwarting of a crime[...] Evaluators live at the desk. They pass questions to the providers: Why is X no longer chairman? They transform the information that the providers produce into analytical notes [...] It would be wrong to imagine the providers and the evaluators as a team. Evaluators are not supposed to know informants' identities, providers cannot read the evaluations of the evaluators. They should not influence each other. Providers deliver pieces of a jigsaw [puzzle], evaluators put them together to form a picture. Superiors pass on the picture to policemen, prosecutors, civil servants in the Ministry of the Interior. (Musharbash 2013)

What does that mean for the production of knowledge?

A product delivered

Politicians, the public and the administration expect the *Verfassungsschutz* to provide an overview of groups and tendencies that threaten civil order in the Federal Republic. The Ämter are expected to provide information on the activities of foreign powers on the territory of the Federal Republic (such as espionage) and map the activity of left-wing, right-wing and Islamist extremists. A PowerPoint presentation by the *Verfassungsschutzamt* of

North Rhine-Westphalia (VNR-W), entitled "Islam and Islamism. Attributes and Developments", produced around 2005 for a public audience, is a good example of how the agency tries to do justice to this expectation.[6] Figures 1a and 1b show how the VNR-W estimated the danger emanating from various Islamist groups, which it is required to do by its mandate.

Figure 1a: Risks according to the readiness to use violence.

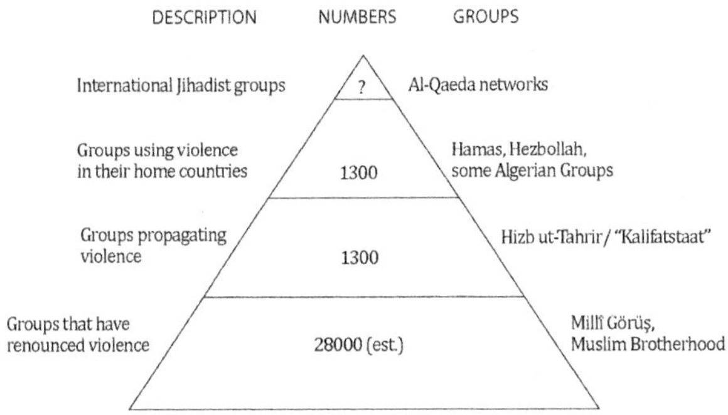

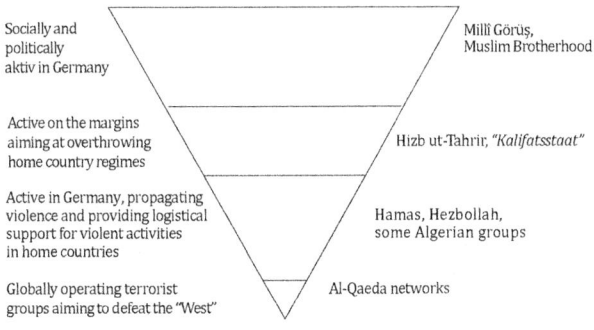

DESCRIPTION	NUMBERS	GROUPS
International Jihadist groups	?	Al-Qaeda networks
Groups using violence in their home countries	1300	Hamas, Hezbollah, some Algerian Groups
Groups propagating violence	1300	Hizb ut-Tahrir / "Kalifatstaat"
Groups that have renounced violence	28000 (est.)	Millî Görüş, Muslim Brotherhood

Figure 1b: Risks arranged according to long-term effects (adapted from "Islam and Islamism. Attributes and developments" [VNR-W 2007-8]).

Socially and politically aktiv in Germany	Millî Görüş, Muslim Brotherhood
Active on the margins aiming at overthrowing home country regimes	Hizb ut-Tahrir, *"Kalifatsstaat"*
Active in Germany, propagating violence and providing logistical support for violent activities in home countries	Hamas, Hezbollah, some Algerian groups
Globally operating terrorist groups aiming to defeat the "West"	Al-Qaeda networks

---

6 It has meanwhile been taken off the internet, probably because it was too revealing of state activities.

Although outdated (Salafism, very prominent today, did not then figure), it illustrates the kind of knowledge relating to Islam created in the *Verfassungsschutzämter*. It is also good for thinking about connections between ethos and knowledge production.

Knowledge about extremist Islamist groups is arranged in two pyramids according to the size and nature of the risk posed by each group. The presentation translates statements, which were contained in the annual reports, into a scheme. Fig 1a depicts short-term dangers resulting from acts of violence, while Fig 1b depicts long-term dangers for the societal order. Thus the configuration of the map displays the nature and size of the risk.

At the base of the pyramids, one finds violence-abjuring Islamist groups such as Millî Görüş or the Muslim Brotherhood, which are included because they supposedly work to overthrow the German constitution by legal means. Right above them are groups such as Hizb ut-Tahrir and the *"Kalifatstaat"*, which are nonviolent in Germany but promote the use of violence to liberate their respective homelands. Next come groups participating in armed struggles in their respective homelands, including Hamas and Hezbollah. At the apex, internationally operating terrorists such as Al-Qaeda are represented. The overall idea expressed in juxtaposing the two pyramids is that Millî Görüş and the Muslim Brotherhood pose the least risk with regard to violent attacks but the highest with regard to long-term effects on the societal order; whereas exactly the reverse is true for Al-Qaeda: It presents the greatest risk from terrorist attacks but the least risk relating to societal order.

A number of aspects of this representation deserve attention. First, it is limited to Islamist groups, which are distinguished from Islamic communities. According to the *Verfassungsschutz*, Islam is "religion" in the true sense, whereas Islamism is ideology, namely the "abuse of the religion of Islam for the political aims and purposes of the Islamists".[7] Since Islam as a religion is protected by the constitution, it does not appear in this classification. Second, the categories used to classify groups (nonviolent, violent, etc.) are derived for a very specific perspective, namely, the security of the German nation state. Methodological nationalism structures the presentation. Of course, this is the perspective state agencies have to take, but it must be remembered because there is a marked tendency to forget the positionality of the insights. Thirdly, groups active in Germany are sorted into

---

7 Bundesamt für Verfassungsschutz 2019.

different risk categories – Millî Görüş[8] and the Muslim Brotherhood are categorised as "renouncing violence" and "socially and politically active groups in Germany", while Hizb-ut Tahrir and the Caliphate State[9] find themselves labelled as "propagating violence", and "active on the margins of local society and struggling to overthrow regimes at home". Thus, the point of view taken differs systematically from one that, for example, a student of Islamic religion would assume, who, aiming at an emic view, might sort them according to schools of theological reasoning or according to genealogy.

The representation is a fine example of the form of state knowledge as a whole. In his lectures on the state, Pierre Bourdieu described the creation of official, public categories, which are generally accepted as valid, as a central act of statehood (2014: 33.34). Homogenous, quantifiable, static and bounded units are created and arranged. With such maps, society is made legible (Scott 1998).

Other authorities (such as integration offices) need and demand this type of knowledge in order to carry out their duties. The 2007-8 PowerPoint presentation acknowledges this by assigning specific administrative strategies to individual categories. While Al-Qaeda is to be fought using military means "such as the destruction of camps and weapons, targeted killing or arrest of fighters and supporters" (VNR-W 2007-8: slide 30), groups using violence in their home counties or otherwise propagating violence should be outlawed (VNR-W 2007-8: slides 31, 32), and groups operating seemingly within the law (which the *Verfassungsschutz* refers to, somewhat misleadingly, as "legalistic Islamist organisations") should be repressed using methods such as tax audits and investigations (VNR-W 2007-8: slide 33).

In *Verfassungsschutz* reports, the same categories that structure the representation of Islamism also structure the representation of right- and left-wing extremism. In all these domains, distinctions are made between groups that reject violence and work politically within society, and groups that directly confront society. Symmetry in representation is made possible by the concept of extremism. Following Backes and Jesse (1996), extremism is seen by the *Verfassungsschutz* as a "collective term for various political endeavours, which share the rejection of the democratic constitutional state and its fundamental values and rules of play" (Verfassungsschutzbericht

---

8 For Millî Görüş, see Schiffauer 2010.
9 For the "*Kalifatstaat*", see Schiffauer 2000.

Berlin 2009: 144). This underlying worldview can be represented by several concentric circles. The centre of society is surrounded by a sphere of "soft" extremism (Jesse 2008), within nested spheres of tougher, more violent extremisms. Danger to society comes from the extremist edges.

This theory is attractive to state apparatuses for several reasons. It allows equal treatment of different groups, thus reinforcing the ethos of neutrality and the impartiality of state action. It identifies the State with the "centre of society" and thus stages its centrality. More practically, the theory of extremism assigns answers to threats developed on an earlier field of conflict (let's say, the fight against leftist radicalisation during the seventies) to threats emerging on other fields. The usual sequence of analysis and strategy development is turned upside down: strategy does not follow analysis, but analysis follows strategy. In other words, if strategies of policing have proven successful, it is tempting to organise knowledge production in a manner that fills the same primary categorical distinctions. The role of analysis, then, becomes less of a guide for strategy development, and more of a means to legitimise and rationalise existing strategies.

Translating the territory onto a map

Like all maps, the map discussed here reduces complexity. However, it is important to know what happens to raw data processed according to *Verfassungsschutz* ethics and ethos. Following Latour, I conceive of knowledge production as a multi-step process, in which concrete, object-oriented knowledge is elaborated upon and transformed in several steps, until it becomes cartographic, tabular or statistical knowledge in the end. In this process of reworking, the concreteness and abundance of low-level knowledge are lost. What is gained, however, is comparability and an overview. Latour conceived of this step-by-step reduction and abstraction as a translation process. In our case the steps of translation are from (1) the informant's oral report to the provider's written protocol, to (2) the evaluator's text, drawn from various sources, to (3) the synoptic representation that gives an abstract overview. Following Latour, our analysis consists of determining what is saved and what is lost at every transition. By focusing on translation, Latour places the discontinuities in data processing at the centre of the investigation. None of these steps follows automatically. Each requires conscious decision-making and active intervention.

Awareness of these transformation chains is crucial in understanding acquired knowledge. Latour insists that it is impossible to relate the final product of cognitive work – the maps, diagrams, and classifications – directly to the raw components (e.g. Latour 2014: 119 ff). Rather, one must revisit the chain of successive translations step by step. By conceiving of the process this way, he takes an intermediate position between a correspondence-theoretical realism and a constructivism that renounces truth-claims. Applying this insight to our field, we observe that an official report is neither: it is not matter of fact, nor is it deliberate construction. An analysis of the translation processes carried out when producing the reports allows us to understand the specific nature of the knowledge created.

To adequately grasp these processes, one would have to carry out participant observation among *Verfassungsschutz* officials similar to the research Bruno Latour carried out among the pedologists of Boa Vista (Latour 1999). As few other sectors in society are as secretive as the public sector (and intelligence services in particular), this is impossible. I suggest an alternative route that contrasts the *Verfassungsschutz*' scrutiny of the Islamic landscape from above and from a distance with an anthropologist's view from nearby and from the side. This is the view of an educated and trained participant observer. By contrasting the result of participant observation[10] with the map, we learn what is kept and what is lost during data processing.

Five reductions of complexity can be observed. The first concerns the internal plurality of the Islamic communities. When viewed from nearby, they no longer appear homogeneous. Rather, one gets the impression of arenas of intense discussion, with different factions striving to position their community in society at large and determine the course to pursue. The subtext of the debates is mostly the dilemma of continuity and change,[11] which is particularly intense in immigrant communities. Most comprehend that continuity is only possible through change – but one must avoid petrification,

---

10 Apart from my own research on Islamic communities in Germany (Schiffauer 2000, 2010) I refer to Klinkhammer (2000), Frese (2002) Jonker (2002, 2005, 2006), Tezcan (2002) and Thielmann (2013, 2014). While these scholars differ in their theoretical outlook, they agree on the empirical findings discussed here.

11 This is a basic problem for religions in general. See Ernst Troeltsch (1977/1925) and Latour (2014: 85ff.).

on the one hand, and self-abandonment on the other. However, the need to achieve this balance in specific areas is controversial. Questions arise in terms of sexual morality and family ethics, political engagement and theological positioning, to name but a few contentious areas. One can observe that a conservative attitude towards sexual ethics does not necessarily correspond to a conservative attitude with regard to politics or theology.[12]

There are some attempts by the *Verfassungsschutz* to do justice to heterogeneity at the community level by introducing "cartographic" sub-divisions. For example, "traditionalists" were at one time distinguished from "reformers" within Millî Görüş; another time there was the attempt to differentiate "fundamentalism" from "extremism/Islamism" (Puschnerat 2006: 219). Nevertheless, such distinctions are too clumsy to do justice to the complexities of negotiation. This is because while categorisations may become more elaborate, they are not dynamic – no matter how intricate the category system becomes, it will always remain rigid. It freezes positions which are in a state of flux. Moreover, compulsory final evaluations are to be made in order to arrive at unequivocal policy recommendations. They necessitate the withdrawal of distinctions introduced earlier in order to make unambiguous knowledge available to decision-making authorities. Certainty is restored. An example of a summarising evaluation may illustrate this:

> Even if some reformers demand a reorientation of Millî Görüş-IGMG, key protagonists still stick to the dogmatic ideals of the original Millî Görüş. It is therefore doubtful whether reforms can be implemented in the organisation or made sustainable. (Verfassungsschutzbericht, 2009: 34)

The quotation shows how distinctions that were introduced (in this case, the demand for reform), are ultimately withdrawn. They remain, but are irrelevant to the overall assessment. The homogeneity thus reproduced has far-reaching consequences. When an IGMG member applied for citizenship, the application was generally denied. It was argued that individual members of an organisation hostile to the constitution could be held responsible for

---

12 The post-Islamist generation in Millî Görüş communities may serve as an example: their members are religious, frequently stricter than their parents, and at the same time politically more open to the secular rule of law and democracy than their parents (Schiffauer 2010: 158-225).

the group doctrine. An exception was made only if the applicant could convincingly prove membership of the reformist wing. Thus, the burden of proof was laid on the applicant.

In this context, the rhetoric of numbers deserves attention. A central function of categorisation is to facilitate quantification. Digitisation is a central technique of governmentality (Porter 2015): only what can be expressed numerically "counts" in politics. Every child learns at school that apples and pears should not be counted together unless they are grouped as "fruit". Numbers imply homogeneity, uniformity. They play a crucial role in risk assessment, in evaluation procedures, and in justifying interventions. If the number of members of a category, such as that of "legalistic Islamist organisations", is set at 2900 (in Berlin), readers assume that 2900 individuals have corresponding orientations. In this context, the 2014 report of the Verfassungsschutz carried out a telling turnaround. It states that:

> Meanwhile, some IGMG supporters in Berlin are no longer pursuing extremist goals. Overall, a process of change is to be seen, which shows a growing distance from the extremist ideology of [Necmettin] Erbakan. Internal positions are increasingly occupied by reform-oriented officials. To take this into account, we no longer judge the IGMG as a whole to be extremist, but only those who hold the extremist, "Millî Gorus" ideology. Berlin's *Verfassungsschutz* therefore focuses on those organisations and aspirations whose aims are the implementation of the "Millî Görüş" ideology. This reduces the potential ["legalistic Islamists", WS] in Berlin from 2900 individuals in the IGMG to the 500 IGMG members who support the Millî Görüş movement. (Verfassungsschutzbericht Berlin 2014:66)

Obviously, this drastic change in assessment from one year to the next does not correspond to a sudden reshuffling in organisational membership. Rather, it reflects a gradual, long-term shift that was not represented in the reports for many years. Only when the old figures were no longer tenable was the assessment abruptly re-adjusted.

Constructing indices of attribution is another knowledge problem of sociological interest.[13] As a rule, a verbal statement favouring Erbakan or an

---

13 On the anthropology of indices, see Rottenburg et al., 2015.

affirmative reference to Qaradawi[14] (for example, in the context of the European Council for Fatwa and Research) can assign a subgroup or individuals to the "legalistic" group within Millî Görüş. We can observe a double reduction of complexity. On the one hand, people holding a wide range of positions are reduced to a single position (Erbakan on *Adil Düzen* [*Just Order*],[15] Qaradawi on his fatwa related to suicide bombings). On the other hand, the variety of reasons that may inspire personal or group admiration are not taken into account. Someone may revere Erbakan for purely religious reasons, while disregarding his political work. Such veneration may well be compatible with a deeply democratic spirit.

Reduction of complexity also occurs when boundaries are crosscutting and overlap. A close look shows that boundaries between Islamic organisations are anything but clear. In fact, local differences are sometimes greater than disparities between umbrella organisations. By no means is a "liberal spirit" or "greater worldliness" more common in a DİTİB community[16] than in a Millî Görüş community. At close range, seemingly clear boundaries dissolve and are replaced by continuities, overlaps and transitions.

The clear boundary the *Verfassungsschutz* draws between Islam (religion) and Islamism (political ideology) is by no means as distinct as the *Amt* suggests. The question of how far religion is political – and must be political – cannot easily be answered. It constitutes an open search leading to provisional answers. Religions put God, man, nature and society in a relationship that cannot be reduced to a private relationship between God and the believer. Yet, all religions define worldly tasks from their basic understanding of these relationships. Many believers are faced by the dilemma of how much

---

14 Yusuf Abdallah al-Qaradawi is an Islamic legal scholar, television preacher and author. In the context of the "European Council for Fatwa and Research", he has spoken out for the further development of Islamic jurisprudence in order to into take account the situation in Europe. From an internal Islamic perspective, he is seen as one of the legal scholars practicing a liberal interpretation of Islamic law (Caeiro 2003 and Schiffauer 2010, 233ff., on the relationship between Millî Görüş and the Council). Qaradawi became a target of the *Verfassungsschutz*, because he defended suicide bombings in Palestine, arguing that otherwise an equality of arms would not exist (Schiffauer 2010: 237).

15 Adil Düzen: "Just Order" is a document in which Necmettin Erbakan laid down his vision of an Islamic state in 1993. For more on Adil Düzen, see Schiffauer 2010: 69ff.

16 The DİTİB is an Islamic umbrella organisation affiliated with the State Office of Religious Affairs (DIYANET) of the Turkish Republic. Officially it stands for a secular interpretation of Islam.

compromise can be made in dealing with the world. Where must one draw the line? Like the aforementioned dilemma of continuity and change, this challenge opens up ways of manoeuvring between an ethics of responsibility (*Verantwortungsethik*) and an ethics of conscience (*Gesinnungsethik*),[17] and leads to novel – usually provisional – answers that may redefine community boundaries. One example is a movement in the Millî Görüş community away from what I called populist Islamism towards a mainly post-Islamist religious community (Schiffauer 2010). Here, the relationship to the world was constantly renegotiated. Of course, some communities emphasise the borders that separate them from the outside, maintaining an internal cohesion and consciously creating a far-reaching consensus.[18] However, these communities are minoritarian. Most Muslim believers would condemn them as sectarian, since the emphasis on boundaries is divisive and abhorrent to the Islamic quest for unity.

State authorities' desire for clear boundaries also reflects a widespread fear of public scandals or legal objections. The need to justify political decisions leads to a tendency to emphasise the boundaries between categories, and to exaggerate the differences between them. If a politician "categorically" refuses an invitation by a particular organisation, he has to give good reasons as to why he makes this distinction. The "legalist", violence-advocating, or violence-promoting categories of Islamism must be clearly distinguished so that differential treatments can be justified and will stand up in court decisions. In other words, political reasons require "discriminatory distinctions" (Farschid 2015: 143). These political considerations, however, have to remain hidden, and it is instead claimed that these distinctions arise from the nature of things.

Another reduction of complexity relates to the apprehension of temporality. We have already discussed this in the context of homogenisation. Categorical knowledge is sluggish. This is probably due to the fact that categorical knowledge produces fixed "identities". Categorical thinking starts with continuity and considers change as exceptional or requiring an explanation. This differs from hermeneutic-procedural thinking, which takes its depar-

---

17 The dilemma between an ethics of responsibility and an ethics of conscience was developed by Max Weber in his essay on "Politics as profession" (*Politik als Beruf*) (1919/1994).
18 See, e.g. my description of the *"Kalifatstaat"* (Schiffauer 2000).

ture from change, and considers the emergence of continuity or the consolidation of "identities" as phenomena requiring explanation.

As mentioned above, complexity reduction also results from the symmetrical treatment of different kinds of extremisms. Criticism of the distortions that arise from the analogous treatment of left- and right-wing extremisms has recently been voiced, especially by left-wing social scientists.[19] In this context, the distortions are even greater when the categorical apparatus is applied to Islamism. This is because left-wing and right-wing extremisms are secular movements, whereas Islamism is grounded in religion. The motivations, debates, and developmental logic of Islamism cannot be understood when it is marked as a "political ideology". Here, too, it suffices to illustrate this with a single example: if one takes Islamism as a political ideology, one considers the ramifications of the Muhammad cartoons essentially from the standpoint of political mobilisation. The Islamist appears to "instrumentalise" and "abuse" religious feelings. The fact of a genuinely felt religious harm is withdrawn from consideration and is no longer seen as a motive for political action.

Finally, complexity reduction results from the imperative to make findings public. This implies accountability. The *Verfassungsschutz* has to justify why it observes one group but not another with a similar outlook. In order to legitimise and rationalise decision-making, the office must stress the differences between them. Idiosyncrasies become emphasised as essential attributes. This has to be done in a manner that withstands court challenges. In other words: groupings are made more different than they appear on ground. Continuities that exist in reality are replaced by discontinuities.

To summarise: When processing the data in order to map the field of Islamic communities, the *Verfassungschutz* saves the content but discards the structure. All the positions mentioned in the reports exist; the problem lies in sorting them into fixed categories. In the translation process, an extremely complex, heterogeneous and dynamic field comes to be represented in a static map. That which is fluid is fixed; the porous is made water-tight; the heterogenous made homogenous. In short, a categorical fiction is produced.

Differences between bureaucratic and everyday knowledge have been emphasised by other ethnographers of state apparatuses, notably James Scott (1998), David Graeber (2015) and Michael Herzfeld (1993). All three

---

19 See the debate in *Politik und Zeitgeschehen*, Heft 47/2008.

formulate a sweeping criticism of bureaucratic knowledge and demand its replacement with practical knowledge, *metis* (Scott), or hermeneutics (Graeber). What they do not see is that categorical knowledge cannot be replaced by other forms of knowledge because it is (also) an expression of administrative rationality. State action requires categorical knowledge to fulfil the state's mandate to carry out and enforce decisions that have been reached democratically. There is no administration without categorisation. Hermeneutical knowledge does play a role in administrative practice: it comes into play in discretionary practice,[20] or in potential challenges to administrative decisions. But doing justice to individual cases must remain the exception in administrative practice. It is time consuming, costly and inefficient.

Categorical knowledge is also required when security issues are involved. While hermeneutical knowledge allows qualitative insights (for example, into the nature of radicalisation), it cannot be used to estimate how many violent Islamists are around. Although it concedes that there *are* violent Islamists, it insists that the phenomenon cannot be clearly defined and that numbers are illusionary. This type of knowledge does not allow the administration of security, nor the planning or legitimisation of security measures.

Categorical knowledge is thus double faced – it permits repression, on the one hand, but limits government action, on the other. The principle of proportionality, crucial for security policy in the democratic state, cannot be based on hermeneutical knowledge that emphasises transitions and processes. Ultimately, with a security policy based on hermeneutical knowledge, anybody or nobody could come under suspicion. Categorical knowledge, by contrast, promises to limit, isolate and then "combat" problematic phenomena in an almost surgical manner. For good or bad, security agencies focus on some, but leave the rest in (relative) peace. Finally, hermeneutic knowledge makes it very difficult to establish legal responsibilities and accountability. Thus, categorical knowledge undergirds state governance and the maintenance of social order. When the ability to distinguish and to differentiate disappears, totalitarianism results.

Much of governance is based on categorical fictions. One must act "as if" it were possible to draw clear boundaries and separate categories. The issue is not to do away with the maps, as Scott and Graeber demand, but rather, to

---

20 This has been intensively discussed in the literature on street-level bureaucracy (Lipsky 1980, Evans and Harris 2004, Hupe 2013, Buffat 2015, Evans 2015).

reflect on the process of knowledge production out of which a map is produced. Awareness of this "as if", of the contingent character of the knowledge base, is crucial for good administrative practice. Only if civil servants apprehend that the map is not the territory will they avoid problematic and unintended consequences. This, however, is difficult, as I will show in the next section.

Five mechanisms for confusing the map and the territory

Five mechanisms work to conceal the fact that categorical knowledge only partly grasps the complexities and temporalities of facts on the ground.

First, the constructedness of categorical knowledge often escapes its architects. Two aspects seem to be central to this operational blindness. One lies in the practice of boundary-drawing itself. Setting and drawing boundaries are acts of "de-fining" (literally, "setting limits") a phenomenon. One establishes its "essence", what it is, by setting it apart from what it is not. The act of definition is a decisive step towards the essentialisation of the phenomenon. Not only are limits defined, the suggestion is that they relate to substance. This suggestion is reinforced because each definition also structures perception. It constitutes a paradigm (Kuhn 1962/1976) and exhibits all the mechanisms captured so well in Kuhn's analysis. One sees what one expects to see and takes this as a proof that things are actually as represented. But the practical organisation of intelligence work also contributes to operational blindness. The separation of informants, providers and evaluators required by *Verfassungsschutz* ethics may guarantee "objectivity" to some degree, but it also systematically reduces the information that appears in the reports. As evaluators receive only second-hand information, they cannot access the contradictions and complexities that arise in face-to-face interactions. They get no "feel" of the situation, which might help them to question or contextualise indexical clarity.

A second mechanism derives from the interface management required by institutional ethos. The *Verfassungsschutz* does not take on an operational role itself. It "only observes" and informs other authorities, who operate based on knowledge the *Verfassungsschutz* provides. On the one hand, this process limits their offices' field of activity (which is wanted); on the other hand, it solidifies and objectivises knowledge.

Mapmakers – in this case *Verfassungsschutz* evaluators – are at least partly aware of the problems related to mapping. They know what difficulties arise when sorting phenomena into categories transforms continuities into discontinuities; they also understand the difficulties arising when phenomena do not fit. However, this perspective-granting insight disappears when knowledge is transferred to another place.

This became very clear to me when I reconstructed a security hearing held in Munich in 2012 concerning a citizenship application from a member of Millî Görüş. These hearings are required when somebody admits to membership in a group classified as extremist (from a list provided to them) during the application process. A section head (*Sachgebietsleiterin*) in the office responsible for foreigners (*Ausländeramt*), a civil servant who did not belong to the *Verfassungsschutz*, conducted the hearing. She was briefed by a letter from the *Verfassungsschutz* summarising information in the reports. What constituted the endpoint for the *Verfassungsschutz* was the starting point for the interlocutor in charge of the hearing. She had no knowledge of the complex processing of information underlying the summary given to her. The civil servant had to take the statements literally – as a reality upon which to act. On this basis, the security hearing was conducted and developed its own dynamics. The applicant was confronted with "objective" information that portrayed the Milli Görüş as political, whereas she herself had experienced it as religious. Faced with this, she had two choices: either to state that she had been deceived by her co-believers and her first-hand knowledge was wrong, or to insist that all she had seen and experienced in the community was purely religious. She opted for the latter and her testimony was interpreted as the claims of a clever Islamist. How could she not have realised the organisation's political character? The hearing turned into a farce, with its very purpose (to do justice to the specific features of the case) thereby undermined.[21] The case shows how an operational structure based on an ethical principle – the separation of knowledge gathering and official implementa-

---

21 The relevance of this point became particularly clear when she appealed to the courts. In the court hearing, which I was able to attend, it became transparently obvious that the presiding judge was in a situation similar to that of the section head described above. He formed his opinion based on documents prepared by the *Verfassungsschutz*. He was blatantly in the proverbial situation of the blind man hearing a description of the colour red. In this case, the *Verfassungsschutz* representative felt compelled to point out that the specific culture of mosque communities had to be taken into account in order to arrive at

tion – can work in reverse. What was meant as a restriction of *Verfassungsschutz* power (it only observes), in fact reinforces its power of definition. Its knowledge is regarded as absolute because the construction of knowledge has been obscured.

A third mechanism derives from the logic of security politics. The fact that the security services analyse hazards means that information provided by the *Verfassungsschutz* is taken seriously and given great weight. In particular, it is tempting for politicians to accept the *Verfassungsschutz* reports uncritically and act accordingly. If nothing happens, this can be attributed to the implementation of expert recommendations. If something does happen, blame can be laid at the feet of the *Verfassungsschutz*. By making the knowledge provided by the Verfassungsschutz the basis of action, it is solidified and re-affirmed.[22]

The secretiveness that characterises the work of the *Verfassungsschutz* is a fourth, powerful mechanism justified by the fact that "that the office's role in constitutional protection requires it to protect its sources". This may be so, but it also obscures the production of evidence. While other knowledge producers, such as the Federal Office for Migration and Refugees (BAMF) or university departments, generate data from which conclusions are drawn transparently and which are therefore open to review, this is not the case with the *Verfassungsschutz*. The risky translations that guide any process of knowledge production remain hidden. Ultimately, the *Verfassungsschutz* demands unconditional faith in its findings – and thus trust in the state. It is remarkable how well this technique works: reference to esoteric knowledge, accessible only to initiates, triggers a kind of theological reflex. Remarkably, its obscurity increases, rather than diminishes, the willingness to believe it.

Finally, a fifth mechanism relates to the fact that administrative categories are highly self-fulfilling. Individuals and groups subjected to categorisation have very few options other than to play along and thus affirm the labels. Even if they feel they are wrongly represented, they have no effective

---

a proper understanding. He thus pointed out cognitive gaps in the paperwork, of which he was aware, but which were not evident to an outsider.

22 It should be mentioned some prominent politicians, like the former senator of the interior of Berlin, Erhart Körting, criticised this tendency of political actors as a refusal of political responsibility. A negotiation process in which security arguments are weighed against integration arguments and the basis of knowledge from the *Verfassungsschutz* is checked would enhance political responsibility.

alternative but to defend themselves in those terms ("We are not Islamists"), or to partner in dialogues (such as the *Islamkonferenz*) or on boards (like those set up for Islamic Theology). The fact that people who are classified also use the classifications, *nolens volens*, only insisting that they are put in the wrong box, confirms their validity. As everybody agrees on the script, it becomes the basis for interaction and its artificiality tends to be forgotten.

All these mechanisms contribute to the ever-increasing consolidation of *Verfassungschutz* knowledge. In the end, map and territory become indistinguishable. The "as if" character of categorical knowledge remains deeply hidden.

Biopolitical challenges

As long as the state apparatus is administering, surveilling and disciplining, the mapping itself is largely self-affirming. Only when dealing with exceptions, as in discretionary practice, do differences between map and territory become visible. But these exceptions confirm the rule rather than question it.

However, ethical conflicts exist with biopolitically oriented state agencies that see their task less as administrative, and more as focused on finding proactive solutions to societal problems through the organisation of dialogue and participation. Departments and initiatives involved in the area of integration policy do not differ from security agencies in their vision of the common good. But they arrive at other strategies to pursue their aims. While security agencies see their task as surveilling and disciplining, integration agencies see their task as the organisation of *living* together. In this case, they set up a framework for Islamic *life* in Germany. Following Foucault, the logic of integration policies is the logic of control and regulation aimed at bringing forth subjects who rule themselves.[23] State agencies and initiatives active in the field of biopolitics often find the mapping developed by the *Verfassungsschutz* too rigid and misleading.

---

23 This formulation draws heavily on Foucault's work on governmentality and biopolitics. I don't see this in terms of a regime based on surveilling and disciplining being replaced by one characterized by control and regulation. The different techniques work side by side, at least in the security apparatus, however there are tensions between the different logics of governance (Foucault 2006a/2006b).

Examples of biopolitical initiatives concerning Islam in Germany include the Islam Conference (Tezcan 2012), the establishment of Islamic theological programs at universities in the Federal Republic, as well as various deradicalisation policies and all kinds of pedagogical intervention. The idea is to create consensus and identification through dialogue, involvement and persuasion (Friedrich Ebert Foundation 2015). Here, the emphasis on soft control and encouragement implies quite a different ethics and ethos from that of the security agencies. Integration agencies represent a benevolent authoritarianism. Their task is to domesticate. Their ethics and ethos resemble those of good teachers. They are committed to openness, respect and understanding while never forgetting the asymmetrical character of their relationships. They share with the security agencies the conviction that it is necessary to set limits and to be completely clear about what is acceptable and what not. But whereas categorical knowledge is the basis of action for security agencies and qualitative knowledge becomes important when dealing with exceptions, biopolitical approaches reverse this order. They generally rely on qualitative knowledge of the particular; categorical knowledge only comes in play when drawing red lines.

When dealing with Islam, the two ethics clash from time to time. Departments and individuals in charge of integration, for example, are in favour of community initiatives signalling support for an open society. Building up self-regulatory mechanisms is what they're looking for. For example, the project "Isl'amour – hand in hand against forced marriage" by Muslim Youth (2009)[24] was supported by the local District Office of Friedrichshain-Kreuzberg of Berlin, whose civil servants knew the activists personally and assumed that the most effective interventions came from the communities themselves. Despite strong support, the Federal Ministry of Family and Social Affairs rejected their request for funding, arguing that some cooperation partners were listed as extremists in the *Verfassungsschutzbericht* (the Muslim brotherhood and Millî Görüş). What the District Office construed as an argument in favour of the project (initiatives coming from within conservative communities themselves) was a no-go for the security agencies (sup-

---

24 Others include the "Dialogue – Young People for Human Rights" project (2009) and the "Youth against Violence" project (2010) in Braunschweig, which tried to foster cooperation with the police against street violence.

port would blur boundaries and legitimise legalist Islamist organisations). The security agencies had the final say.

Civil servants at the local District Office felt that they were relegated to second-class status and expressed serious dissatisfaction with the procedure. They felt particularly bitter because they received no more detailed knowledge justifying the denial of funding than did their Muslim clients. All they learned was that the two organisations concerned were under surveillance by the *Verfassungsschutz*, information they already possessed. No concrete evidence was given about individuals involved in the project. They felt that the verdict, based on schematic categorical knowledge, stigmatised precisely the group that they had tried to win over for the development of civil society. They argued that promoting these projects would have improved the standing of progressive activists in their communities. Refusal would weaken progressive circles, justifying the views of community members who regard such initiatives as illusionary, "because society does not want Islam anyway". Finally, the civil servants expressed regret that they could not articulate their dissatisfaction about the decision in public. All comments were "off the record".

Conclusion

In this chapter, I have examined knowledge production in the *Verfassungsschutzämter* to show how it is structured by the ethics and ethos of the office as the institutionalisation of *wehrhafte Demokratie*. Taking Islamist communities as my example, I demonstrated that the knowledge produced certainly reflects the landscape of production but reflects it in a special way. It is a scientific-ethical hybrid – and an adequate understanding of it has to take into account its hybridity. It cannot be criticised in a purely scientific way, in terms of the validity and reliability of its insights. If one questions the validity of a clear categorical distinction between Islamism and Islam, one is told that this question is beside the point because there are ethical reasons that necessitate making it and upholding it. Or if one points to distortions arising from the division of work between "providers" and "evaluators", one us informed that the applicable work-ethos discourages seriously questioning this, given the specific historical precedent of the *Gestapo*.

Of course, categorical knowledge has serious shortcomings. It provides static maps of a highly fluid field. This becomes a problem for other state agencies that share the same idea of the common good but derive other strategies – i.e. biopolitical ones – to achieve it. This results in a clash of ethics and ethos among different state agencies. It is the clash between juridico-political ethics and ethos aiming at controlling bodies, and biopolitical-pedagogical ethics and ethos aiming at winning hearts. It would be possible in principle to solve this contradiction by emphasising the constructedness and artificiality of *Verfassungsschutz* knowledge. This is not easy, and we have pointed out the obstacles. The result is, however, that the map is taken as the territory. And this causes state agencies to stumble and trip when it comes to dealing with Muslim communities.

Bibliography

Backes, Uwe and Eckhard Jesse. 1996. *Politischer Extremismus in der Bundesrepublik Deutschland*. Bonn: Propyläen.
Bauman, Zygmunt. 1989/2013. *Modernity and the Holocaust*. Cambridge: Polity Press.
Bourdieu, Pierre. 2014. *Über den Staat*. Berlin: Suhrkamp.
Buffat, Aurelien. 2015. When and why discretion is weak or strong: the case of taxing officers in a Public Unemployment Fund. In Peter Hupe, Michael Hill and Aurelien Buffat, eds, *Understanding Street-Level Bureaucracy*. Bristol: Policy Press.
Bundesamt für Verfassungsschutz. 2019. *Was ist Islamismus?* [online]: https://www.verfassungsschutz.de/de/arbeitsfelder/af-islamismus-und-islamistischer-terrorismus/was-ist-islamismus [accessed 22 August 2019].
Bundesamt für Verfassungsschutz. 2007. *Integration as a means to prevent extremism and terrorism. Typology of Islamist radicalisation and recruitment*. Köln: BfV.
Caeiro, Alexandre. 2003. *The European Council for Fatwa and Research*. Fourth Mediterranean Social and Political Research Meeting, Florenze – Montecatini Terme: Robert Schuman Centre for Advanced Studies.
Eckert, Julia, et al. 2015. *Ethos and Ethics in Migration Bureaucracies*, call for papers, Institut für Sozialanthropologie, Universität Bern.

Evans, Tony and John Harris. 2004. Street-Level Bureaucracy, Social Work and the (Exaggerated) Death of Discretion. *British Journal of Social Work* 43: 871–895.

Evans, Tony. 2015. Professionals and discretion in street-level bureaucracy. In Peter Hupe, Michael Hill and Aurelien Buffat, eds, *Understanding Street-Level Bureaucracy*. Bristol; Policy Press: 279–293.

Farschid, Olaf. 2015. Zur Unterscheidung von Islam und Islamismus. In Dietmar Molthagen, ed., *Handlungsempfehlungen zur Auseinandersetzung mit islamistischem Extremismus und Islamfeindlichkeit*. Berlin: Friedrich-Ebert-Stiftung.

Foucault, Michel. 2006a. Sicherheit, Territorium, Bevölkerung. Geschichte der Gouvernementalität I. Frankfurt am Main: Suhrkamp.

Foucault, Michel. 2006b. *Die Geburt der Biopolitik. Geschichte der Gouvernementalität II*. Frankfurt am Main, Berlin: Suhrkamp.

Frese, Hans-Ludwig. 2002. *Den Islam ausleben. Konzepte authentischer Lebensführung junger türkischer Muslime in der Diaspora*. Bielefeld: transcript.

Friedrich-Ebert-Stiftung. 2015. *Handlungsempfehlungen zur Auseinandersetzung mit islamistischem Extremismus und Islamfeindlichkeit*. edited by Dietmar Molthagen. Berlin: Friedrich-Ebert-Stiftung.

Herzfeld, Michael. 1993. *The Social Production of Indifference. Exploring the Symbolic Roots of Western Bureaucracy*. Chicago, London: University of Chicago Press.

Hupe, Peter. 2013. "Dimensions of Discretion: Specifying the Object of Street-Level Bureaucracy Research." *Der Moderne Staat. Zeitschrift für Public Policy, Recht und Management* 6(2): 425–440.

Jesse, Eckhard. 2008. "Extremistische Parteien" – Worin besteht der Erkenntnisgewinn. *APuZ (Aus Politik und Zeitgeschichte)* (47): http://www.bpb.de/apuz/30841/extremistische-parteien-worin-besteht-der-erkenntnisgewinn-essay?p=all.

Jonker, Gerdien. 2002. *Eine Wellenlänge zu Gott: Der "Verband Islamischer Kulturzentren in Europa"*. Bielefeld: transcript.

Jonker, Gerdien. 2005. The Mevlana Mosque in Berlin-Kreuzberg: An unresolved conflict. *Journal of Ethnic and Migration Studies* 31(6): 1067–1081.

Jonker, Gerdien. 2006. The Generational Change in Milli Görüsh and Jamaatunnur. Religious Responses to the German Security Frame after 9/11. In Gerdien Jonker and Valérie Amiraux, eds, *Strategies of Visibility of young Muslims in European Public Spaces*. Bielefeld: transcript.

Kuhn, Thomas S. 1962/1976. *Die Struktur wissenschaftlicher Revolutionen.* Frankfurt am Main: Suhrkamp.
Latour, Bruno. 1999. Circulating Reference – Sampling the Soil in the Amazon Forest, In Bruno
Latour, Bruno. 1999., *Pandora's Hope: Essays on the Reality of Science Studies.* Cambridge, MA: Harvard University Press: 24–79.
Latour, Bruno. 2014. *Existenzweisen. Eine Anthropologie der Modernen.* Berlin: Suhrkamp.
Lipsky, Michael. 1980. *Street-Level Bureaucracy.* New York: Russell Sage Foundation.
Musharbash, Yassin. 2013. In Heimlichheim. DIE ZEIT, 14 February 2013 [online:] https://www.zeit.de/2013/08/Dossier-Verfassungsschutz-NSU-Terrorismus.
Porter, Theodore. M. 2015. The flight of the indicator. In Richard Rottenburg, Sally E. Merry, Sung-Joon Park and Johanna Mugler, *The World of Indicators. The Making of Governmental Knowledge through Quantification.* Cambridge: Cambridge University Press: 34–55.
Puschnerat, Tania. 2006. Zur Bedeutung ideologischer und sozialer Faktoren in islamistischen Radikalisierungsprozessen – eine Skizze. In Uwe. E. Kemmesies, ed., *Terrorismus und Extremismus – der Zukunft auf der Spur.* München: Luchterhand.
Rottenburg, Richard and Sally E. Merry. 2015. A World of Indicators: The Making of Governmental Knowledge through Quantification. In Richard Rottenburg, Sally E. Merry, Sung-Joon Park and Johanna Mugler, *The World of Indicators. The Making of Governmental Knowledge through Quantification.* Cambridge: Cambridge University Press: 1–33.
Schiffauer, Werner. 2000. *Die Gottesmänner. Türkische Islamisten in Deutschland.* Frankfurt am Main: Suhrkamp.
Schiffauer, Werner. 2010. *Nach dem Islamismus. Eine Ethnographie der Islamischen Gemeinschaft Milli Görüs.* Berlin: Suhrkamp.
Schiffauer, Werner, Gerd Baumann, Riva Kastoryano, und Steven Vertovec. 2002. *Civil Enculturation. Nation-State, School and Ethnic Difference in The Netherlands, Britain, Germany and France.* New York, Oxford: Berghahn.
Scott, James C. 1998. *Seeing like a state: How certain schemes to improve the human condition have failed.* New Haven, CT: Yale University Press.

Tezcan, Levent. 2002. Inszenierungen kollektiver Identität. Artikulationen des politischen Islam – beobachtet auf den Massenveranstaltungen der türkisch-islamischen Gruppe Milli Görüs. *Soziale Welt*, 53(3): 301–322.

Thielmann, Jörn. 2013. Islamic fields and Muslim techniques of the self in a German context. In Samuel M. Behloul, Susanne Leuenberger, Andreas Tunger-Zanetti, eds, *Debating Islam. Negotiating Religion, Europe, and the Self*. Bielefeld: transcript: 203–220.

Thielmann, Jörn. 2014. Islamic Salvation Front. In Emad El-Din Shahin, ed. in chief, *The Oxford Encyclopedia of Islam and Politics*. vol. 1, New York: Oxford University Press: 599–601.

Tietze, Nikola. 2001. *Islamische Identitäten. Formen muslimischer Religiosität junger Männer in Deutschland und Frankreich*. Hamburg: Hamburger Edition HIS.

Troeltsch, Ernst. 1977/1925. *Die Soziallehren der christlichen Kirchen und Gruppen*. Aalen: Scientia Verlag.

Verfassungsschutzbericht Berlin 2009. Berlin. Senatsverwaltung für Inneres und Sport. Abteilung Verfassungsschutz.

Verfassungsschutzbericht Berlin 2013. Berlin. Senatsverwaltung für Inneres und Sport. Abteilung Verfassungsschutz.

Verfassungsschutzbericht Berlin 2014. Berlin. Senatsverwaltung für Inneres und Sport. Abteilung Verfassungsschutz.

Wallace, David Foster. 2011. *The Pale King*. New York: Little, Brown and Company.

Weber, Max. 1919/1974. Der Beruf zur Politik. In Johannes Winckelmann, ed., *Max Weber: Soziologie, Universalgeschichtliche Analysen, Politik*. Stuttgart: Alfred Kröner: 167–185.

Governing the Boundaries of the Commonwealth
The Case of So-Called Assisted Voluntary Return Migration

David Loher

Introduction[1]

In recent years, programmes for so-called assisted voluntary return migration (AVR) have become an important pillar of European migration policy (Broeders 2010).[2] These programmes target asylum seekers whose chances of admission are considered to be low and, in some cases, rejected asylum seekers. They provide advice and financial incentives with the aim of persuading these people to agree to return to their countries of origin. A growing number of studies of migration policy have evaluated and measured the effectiveness of these programmes (e.g. Gosh 2000; International Organization for Migration 2004; Black and Gent 2006; Geiger 2009; Black et al. 2011). However, few studies have attempted to understand the underlying structures and logics of this specific form of migration management, which oscillate between deportation and the provision of assistance on humanitarian grounds (cf. Hammond 1999; Blitz et al. 2005; Webber 2011; Lietaert et al. 2016).

This chapter discusses the logics of these programmes through an analysis of the self-representations of counsellors who work in Switzerland's return migration bureaucracy. It approaches these self-representations not

---

1 This chapter is based on my PhD research project on the governance of clandestine Tunisian migration in the context of Switzerland's assisted voluntary return migration programme. The research was supported by the Swiss Scientific National Foundation SNSF.

2 In this chapter, the term AVR refers to a specific form of migration management in the form of these government programmes. It does not imply consent or agreement with the purported voluntary nature of these programmes.

primarily as individual expressions of personal attitudes, but rather as a reflection of the conflicting bureaucratic ethics that provide moral legitimisation for concrete bureaucratic practices. Whereas several studies have highlighted the messy, conflicting reality of migration bureaucracy and its domination by various interests and actors (e.g. Eule 2014; Cabot 2013), I also see the effects of a structural incommensurability between bureaucracy's universal promises and the governance of commonwealth boundaries. An ideal-typical bureaucracy serves for the benefit of everyone. The critical question is therefore: Who is part of the commonwealth and included in "everyone"? Usually this question is beyond the scope of bureaucracies and allocated to the realm of politics in a Rancièrian sense (see Rancière 1999). In the case of migration bureaucracies, however, structural incommensurability occurs because the object of administration is precisely the formation and delimitation of the commonwealth, and this undermines bureaucracy's universalistic claim. The structural incommensurability of migration bureaucracy generates its necessarily exclusionary logics.

AVR operates against a backdrop of – and often hand in hand with – forced deportation. Since its success depends on the threat of coercion, there is a permanent need to legitimate AVR and to position it in the field of migration management in relation to forced deportation. In order to explore these tensions, I focus primarily on the self-representations of return migration bureaucrats. These officials are well aware that "deportability" (de Genova 2002) is indispensable for AVR as a whole as well as for their individual professional success. At the same time, they assume an ambivalent stance towards coercive measures: either they consider each forced deportation to be a failed AVR, and therefore as a professional failure, or they obfuscate the relationship between AVR and forced deportation. In the latter case, officials argue that they are only consultants, independently and objectively informing their clients – i.e. the migrants – about their rights, duties, constraints and opportunities.

In the first part of this chapter, I discuss the notion of bureaucratic ethics, asking in what ways the ethics of migration bureaucracies differ from the ethics of other bureaucracies. The second part explores the context of AVR, and how this specific field within migration bureaucracy as a whole operates at the intersection between coercion and voluntariness. The third part focuses on the self-representations of return migration bureaucrats in Switzerland and shows via ethnographic analysis how their self-representations relate to different bureaucratic ethics. Finally, I return to the paradox of voluntariness based on coercion and link it to the conflicting bureaucratic ethics of return migration bureaucrats, which causes the structural incommensurability between bureaucracy's universal promise and the administration of commonwealth boundaries.

This chapter draws on ethnographic material I collected between 2012 and 2016 during my PhD research project on the governance of clandestine Tunisian migration in the context of Switzerland's assisted voluntary return migration programme. My research reconstructs the transnational trajectories of Tunisian migrants – so-called *harragas* – confronted with governmental attempts to organise transnational mobility via AVR programmes.[3] In this chapter, I focus on interviews with representatives of five return migration offices in different cantons in Switzerland. Additional observations and analysis of documents help to clarify the logics of the return migration bureaucracy.

Bureaucratic ethics and the specific case of migration bureaucracies

Setting aside the debate on Weber's bureaucratic ethos (see Weber 1922: 655ff; Eckert this volume) – interpreted either as imbued with ethics (see du Gay 2008), or potentially becoming devoid of ethics (e.g. Arendt 1995, Bauman 1989; Habermas 1988; Bayertz 1995: 35f) – I address the question of ethics by examining the aims and values that migration bureaucracies strive to uphold. This approach follows the notion of bureaucracy in Bear and Mathur (2015), who identify two prominent characteristics: the administration of public goods and the pursuit of a utopian social order.

---

3 The term *harraga* is widely used in Tunisia and other North African countries, where it refers to the high-risk migration strategy of crossing the Mediterranean clandestinely in small fishing boats. Harraga has a number of different meanings: On the one hand, it denotes the act of clandestine migration by boat. At the same time, it refers to people who perform the "harraga". The term literally means "burning" or "those who burn", implying a clandestine border crossing ("burning the border"), the people who cross the border, or the act of destroying one's personal papers during the clandestine crossing, a common practice to conceal one's identity from state authorities.

Bureaucracies are also expressions of an implicit social contract between citizens and officials. According to Bear and Mathur, they share four main elements. First, bureaucracies geared towards the public good work by promoting goods and services in the commonwealth according to predefined sets of rules. Second, a delineated commonwealth has the legitimate right to participate in the public good governed by the bureaucracies. In most cases, this right is expressed in the notion of the citizen (see Ferguson 2015).[4] Third, the definition of citizen mediates the relationship between individuals and officials, who enact the relationship between individuals and the state. And finally, bureaucratic practice is oriented towards an imagined utopian social order. This last element contains normative aspects and tells us how society should be. For the interpretation of migration bureaucracies, this last aspect is of particular importance.

Migration bureaucracies share distinct features that set them apart from other bureaucracies. They are characterised by competing logics and agency turf wars (see Eule 2014; Eule et al. 2017), and by illegibility (Hoag 2010). Even though these aspects can be found in virtually any bureaucracy, they appear to be particularly pronounced in migration bureaucracies. Yet, a further aspect points toward a structural difference. Migration bureaucracies are geared towards the governance of inclusion and exclusion (Tuckett 2018). Thus, its object of governance is the commonwealth itself, and not any public good. It differentiates those who are part of the commonwealth from those who are excluded from it. This creates a unique disposition. Those who are excluded from the commonwealth by the migration bureaucracy are both under its governance, and at the same time removed from its realm and placed beyond its reach due to their excluded status. To illustrate this point, compare the migration bureaucracy to a social welfare bureaucracy: Everyone who is part of the commonwealth is a potential beneficiary of the welfare bureaucracy. Whether one is actually entitled to benefit from the goods and services it governs depends on a series of criteria one has to meet (e.g. lack of income, lack of private wealth, further indications of social vulnerability). However, unlike migration bureaucracies, this differentiation does not question one's inclusion in the commonwealth and entitlement, in principle, to these social welfare goods if predefined criteria are met.

---

4 This resonates with Arendt's (1986) idea of citizenship as the right to have rights, when we include in the notion of the public good not only goods and services, but also rights.

One might object that migration bureaucracy's public good is precisely the entitlement to participate legitimately as a full member of the commonwealth – to share in the public good. However, this argument would introduce a sort of second order of public good. Furthermore, it would conflate the distinction between rights/entitlements and public goods.

In the ethnographic material, the ethics of AVR appear as principles and aims such as "protecting the system against abuses", "enforcing the law", and "governing migration in a humanitarian way". In order to explore this specific character of return migration bureaucracies in more detail, the following sections examine the case of Switzerland's AVR programmes not only as a specific type of bureaucracy, but as a specific area within migration bureaucracies.

Governing return migration: Switzerland's AVR programme for Tunisian asylum seekers

In June 2012, Switzerland launched an AVR programme for Tunisian asylum seekers: the *Länderprogramm Tunesien* (country programme Tunisia).[5] This programme provided financial and professional support to individual and collective return projects for Tunisian asylum seekers. These small-scale economic projects were mainly located in the agricultural sector (sheep and cattle breeding, vegetable growing), the small-scale fishing industry, or in skilled crafts and trades. This AVR programme attempted to respond to the increasing number of Tunisian asylum seekers appearing after the Ben Ali regime in Tunisia fell on 14 January 2011. The ensuing turmoil and crumbling security apparatus opened a window of opportunity for mostly young male Tunisians to leave the country comparatively easily. As so-called *harragas*, they left their homeland clandestinely and reached northern Mediterranean shores in old fishing vessels. From there, they moved northwards. At the same time, earlier Tunisian migrants who were employed in Italy's shadow

---

5 Switzerland has two types of assisted return. The "country programmes" (*Länderprogramm*) provide assistance for a limited period, often consist of relatively generous financial support that may be accompanied by the establishment of support capacities. The other is individual return assistance. With some reservations, any asylum seeker can apply for the latter. In general, individual return assistance provides smaller amounts of financial support with little additional support.

economy joined the migration northwards to escape the consequences of the 2008 global financial crisis, which hit Italy's economy hard. Thus, two groups of Tunisian migrants applied for asylum in Switzerland and surrounding countries, and caused a sharp rise in asylum applications between 2011 and 2013.

June 2012 is often considered the beginning of what has become known as the contemporary migration crisis.[6] The *Länderprogramm Tunesien* responded to this supposed crisis, but earlier AVR programmes had already existed.[7] In institutional terms, they can be traced back to the second half of the 1990s in Switzerland. Before that time, return aid was granted randomly to individual return migrants, with no distinct legal basis.[8] It consisted mainly of unofficial assistance to destitute return migrants in the form of plane tickets or small amounts of money to alleviate individual hardship after their return (Kaser and Schenker 2008).

The attempt to integrate an AVR approach into Switzerland's migration policy is closely linked to the end of the Balkan wars. At that time, Switzerland terminated temporary collective protection for people displaced by war. Suddenly, the thousands of refugees remaining in Switzerland were denied subsidiary protection. Lacking valid residence titles, their stay in Switzerland no longer had a legal basis. The consequence was mass expulsion. In order to ease the situation for individual returnees, but also to facilitate and accelerate returns, an AVR programme to Bosnia and Herzegovina was launched as a pilot project in 1996, with assistance from the International Organisation for Migration (IOM) (Kaser and Schenker 2008: 208).

Since then, Switzerland has implemented more than ten *Länderprogramme*. This includes programmes for Sri Lanka (2000-2004), Angola (2002-2007) and Armenia (2004-2008). Country programmes focus on asylum seekers of a particular nationality for a limited period of time so that a joint effort on the part of the migration bureaucracy may decrease their numbers in the asylum system. One can identify three main reasons why

---

6 The popular crisis discourse, however, is not only questionable, producing a permanent "border spectacle" (de Genova 2013, see also Andersson 2016), it also has a short-term memory. Today, the 2015 "refugee crisis" has already superseded the 2012 "crisis", which, today, is nothing more than a faint memory in public discourse.

7 For an overview of AVR in Europe see also Lietaert et al. (2016).

8 The origins of assisted return migration can be traced back to the year 1959 (Kaser and Schenker 2008).

migration bureaucrats consider AVR as the easiest possible way to expel asylum seekers, illegalised migrants and rejected asylum seekers. AVR does not risk violating the fundamental human rights principle of non-refoulement, as every returnee signs a document stating that he or she "returns voluntarily to the country of origin". This document is bureaucratic evidence of the returnee's free decision to return home. In addition, countries of origin, which are often reluctant to accept their deported citizens, or may even forcibly reject them, are more willing to comply with assisted return. Finally, AVR is less costly than forced deportation.

In recent years, expelling rejected asylum seekers and migrants without residence permits has become a political priority in many European countries. As Broeders (2010) observes, this policy has led to contradictory results: Capacity for administrative detention has increased, while at the same time the effective number of expulsions has stagnated or even fallen (see also Castañeda 2010). This means that the "deportability" (de Genova 2010) of thousands of migrants across Europe does not lower the numbers of undocumented migrants and rejected asylum seekers. Instead, increasing numbers are living in a state of legal uncertainty and the everyday threat of deportation. Assisted return operates precisely in the milieu of this everyday insecurity, offering an end to this precarious and uncertain status. Against the backdrop of forced deportation, assisted voluntary return might become an option worth considering for Tunisian asylum seekers, although it contradicts the initial intentions that motivated their clandestine migration.

The double vocation of return counsellors

Since AVR works against the backdrop of forced deportation, a series of appraisals has argued that AVR, in fact, is nothing more than poorly masked coercion and forced deportation. Instead of replicating this important critique once again, I focus on Switzerland's AVR programmes as a case study, examining return migration bureaucrats' self-representations to explore the tension between voluntariness and coercion that results from competing bureaucratic ethics.

As part of my research on Switzerland's Tunisian AVR programme, I conducted a series of interviews with return counsellors. At the beginning of these conversations, my informants often talked a lot about how they conceive of their own work. It was striking to observe how their self-representation systematically invoked the ideal-type of the Weberian bureaucrat. They described asylum bureaucracy as a machine-like system that processes applications with precision, consistency and impartiality. Their role consisted in keeping the system running as smoothly as possible. This template can be found in the self-representation of any of my informants. But as the conversations unfolded, it quickly became obvious that return migration bureaucracy – in its practice, but also in its very conception – does not correspond to this Weberian ideal at all, as is shown in the following example, reconstructed from my field notes.

I was sitting in one of Switzerland's return migration offices, interviewing two bureaucrats about their work.[9] The office was located on the ground floor in a side wing of the canton's security and police department, sharing its reception area with the migration service *(Migrationsamt)*, who administer bureaucratic affairs relating to foreigners in Switzerland.[10] Decorated with a few posters of unidentifiable foreign destinations, the office faintly resembled a travel agency. In one corner near the entrance, a rack contained AVR information brochures in a number of languages. One of my two informants leafed through a pile of documents he had prepared for our conversation and pulled out an image. It was a flowchart, representing Switzerland's asylum procedure schematically. He handed me the chart, pointing with his pencil to the bottom, and began to explain: "Our task is [to ensure] that asylum seekers with negative [asylum] decisions leave Switzerland." The head of department – also present in the room – added:

> We do not like forced deportations. I am convinced that we all want to avoid forced deportations. Our aim is that every rejected asylum seeker returns voluntarily to his home country. [...] As you know, I am just here to enforce negative decisions. I do not make [asylum] decisions. And I am not part of the police forces. So, I try to convince the migrants for their own sake to return to their country of origin.[11]

---

9 Fieldnotes August 2014, clarifications in brackets by D.L.

10 The *Migrationsamt* is the cantonal migration authority. It is responsible for the registration of the non-national population and executes decisions of the federal State Secretariat for Migration.

11 Interview August 2014, clarifications in brackets by D.L.

During our conversation, the two informants repeated on several occasions that they tried hard to avoid forced deportations. These efforts paid off, the department head proudly explained. His canton's return migration office had had the highest proportion of AVRs to asylum seekers in recent years.

The self-representations of these two informants contain three constitutive elements typical of this field: They highlight their duty to enforce negative asylum decisions; they voice their disapproval of forced deportations, while nonetheless defending them as indispensable; and they stress that they suggest the best possible solutions for the asylum seekers they advise. Yet, the weighting of these three elements varies among return migration bureaucrats. Apart from individual preferences, this variance largely depends on the location of each officer's AVR office within the national migration bureaucracy. This becomes apparent when different cases are compared.

In this particular case, the two informants were both committed to enforcing the rules and considered themselves submissive servants to these rules. They both argued that the AVR office contributes to enforcing decisions made previously within the limits of the authority of the office, yet each officer added nuance in stating his position. The head of department clearly prioritised the need to enforce decisions, yet, as the quote shows, argued that certain enforcement methods are preferable to others. The return counsellor, for his part, deviated from the clear-cut, rule-oriented narrative of his superior and mentioned the importance of working with returnees towards mutual consent.

Strict rule-orientation and as well as the emphasis on mutual consent between bureaucrats and asylum seekers are strong expressions of bureaucratic ethos. They serve as a kind of guideline for bureaucratic procedures. And they show that, although enforcement of negative asylum decisions (i.e. returning rejected asylum seekers to their country of origin) is the unquestioned and ultimate aim of the return migration bureaucracy, decisions can be enforced in different ways, and some ways are better than others. In this context, return migration bureaucrats apparently consider so-called voluntary return morally preferable to forced deportation. This contributes to the moral legitimisation of deportations.

Rule-orientation and the public good

Let me take this argument a step further. Rule-orientation always includes more than just concern about procedure or, to borrow John Rawls' term, procedural justice (Rawls 1999: 73-78; see also Nelson 1980). Bureaucrats believe that reliance on the principle of rule-orientation in everyday bureaucratic practice adds to the public good in substantial ways. This blurs the boundaries between bureaucratic ethos and ethics. Defence of procedural rules and principles via strict adherence can be considered an intrinsic aim of bureaucracy, and, it follows, also as an element of bureaucratic ethics. It is no coincidence that the return migration bureaucrat quoted in the previous example refers to a flowchart to explain his work. That tool perfectly visualises the key idea of bureaucracy: an unambiguous set of actions and decisions that is rigorously aligned and follows an exact path. Each action and each decision is preceded by a precisely defined previous action or decision, and followed by a precisely defined subsequent action or decision. The two core principles of bureaucracy represented in the flowchart are hierarchisation and the division of labour (see Handelman 2004). In short, the flowchart is the perfect image of the Weberian ideal-type of bureaucracy.

When asked why this rule-following principle is so important, return counsellors often link it to the issue of fairness. Or, as another informant puts it:

> It would be unfair to those who accept a negative asylum decision, if at the same time others resist and are rewarded for their misconduct, in the sense that they can remain [in the country]. Therefore, it is important to enforce negative decisions.[12]

Identifying the principle of rule-orientation with fairness indicates that more is at stake than concerns about pure procedure. Not enforcing a negative asylum decision is considered unfair towards rejected asylum seekers who accepted their decision and left the country. By this reasoning, rendering justice to every asylum seeker means that every bureaucratic decision must be enforced, because the scope of fairness includes anyone subjected to certain rules. "Fairness" – in the emic meaning captured in the quote –

---

12 Interview August 2014, clarification in brackets by D.L.

corresponds in each case to the idea of coherence throughout the system. This means that each individual case is treated exactly the same as all other cases with the same characteristics, and that sameness makes the system as a whole coherent. Here, the scope transcends the individual case to focus on migration bureaucracy as a whole.

These emic ideas of fairness and coherence contradict a familiar critique of bureaucracy which argues that such a strong sense of commitment to rules – as identified in the statement above – implies simultaneous de-responsibilisation. Commitment to rules does not lead to de-responsibilisation from the bureaucrat's perspective. On the contrary, return migration bureaucrats take the rules seriously precisely because they feel deeply responsible for the commonwealth, and thus insist on the coherence of the decisions.

However, defending the principle of rule-orientation does not imply that return migration bureaucrats agree with the rules they are enforcing. They are well aware that these rules might in some cases lead to questionable results. Some civil servants even criticise the actual migration laws more or less explicitly.[13] They defend rule-orientation by arguing that it guarantees equal treatment to every asylum seeker. In other words, they draw a sharp distinction between the defence of a procedural principle and justifying the actual rules as such. Yet the ethnographic data shows that, in general, return migration bureaucrats only criticise the rules they enforce as private individuals, not in their official roles. This highlights the mode of operation of the bureaucratic principle, which disconnects the private from the official, as Weber (1999) notes. It prioritises rule-following – and therefore procedural or formal justice – over substantive justice. Openly criticising a decision made previously would be judged unprofessional, unless this decision is the outcome of a violation of bureaucratic rules.

The idea that the rule-following principle is worth defending contains a further aspect. Return migration bureaucrats argue that the rule-following principle and the enforcement of negative asylum decisions is "for the benefit of everyone".[14] This aspect is different from fairness, as Moore reminds us: "Strict rules yield certainty but are sometimes unfair. Equity gives attention

---

13 In most cases, this critique is voiced in informal settings. During the interviews, most of the informants avoided personal critical statements.
14 Interview with a return migration bureaucrat, July 2014.

to fairness and morality, but at the expense of legal certainty" (1972: 53). This aspect of certainty is crucial, as it goes beyond the individual case at stake. Following and enforcing bureaucratic rules correctly and consistently is not only an issue between bureaucrats and those immediately concerned with a certain bureaucratic rule. It contains the idea that defending the rule-following principle has a much broader impact on society as a whole. Bureaucrats understand their everyday practice as a contribution to the public good, as this Weberian-like ideal-type bureaucracy stands for the fundamental principle of justice. As du Gay (2000) argues, neutrality, fairness and equal treatment of cases without regard to person form the indispensable condition of possibility of democracy. This is the bulwark against arbitrariness, injustice and unequal treatment. This self-representation assumes that the rule-following principle contains an intrinsic value worth defending, as it provides the necessary condition of democracy.

As a guiding principle of bureaucrats' everyday practice, strict rule-orientation exhibits a surprising parallel to Weber's distinction between *Gesinnungsethik* (ethics of conviction) and *Verantwortungsethik* (ethics of responsibility) (Weber 1922: 237f). Rule-orientation resembles an ethics of conviction in the sense that it focuses on rules and ignores the outcomes. Therefore, rather than echoing a Bauman-inspired critique of bureaucracy as anethical, the ethnographic material reveals a migration bureaucracy full of ethical considerations, which tend to take the form of an ethics of conviction.

Rule-orientation is not the only principle to which migration bureaucrats' self-representation adheres. The following ethnographic material suggests that the principles of efficiency and humanitarian reason contradict – each in a distinct way – the neat picture of bureaucracy wherein rule-orientation provides an indispensable threshold against arbitrariness and injustice.

Efficiency versus rule-orientation

Efficiency as a second principle of bureaucratic ethos stands in tension with the principle of rule-following path-dependency. I suggest interpreting return migration bureaucracy as an institutionalised deviation from strict rule-orientation. In contrast to the dominant mode of self-representation of virtually all return counsellors, the return migration bureaucracy *does not enforce* negative asylum decisions, but *anticipates* such decisions for the simple reason that there are no expulsion orders to enforce – so far at least. The AVR programme for Tunisia explicitly targets Tunisian asylum seekers whose applications are still pending. Why did my interlocutors systematically overlook this obvious paradox?

In conversation, I often asked my informants why they emphasised the rule-following principle, even though AVR operations are obviously *not* in accord with it. In general, their first reaction was incomprehension. Interlocutors rejected my objection as "naïve". They agreed that potential return migrants had not yet received a negative decision on their asylum application when so-called voluntary return was proposed to them, yet my objection seemed "out of touch with reality". One of the two return migration bureaucrats introduced in the first part of this section agreed with his colleagues' assessment of my failure of comprehension. Concerning Tunisian asylum seekers, he argued, it is "obvious" that their asylum applications are "unfounded" and that they will receive a negative decision sooner or later anyway. Another informant explained that, for this reason, his office's policy is to approach every asylum seeker systematically at the "earliest possible moment" in order to disseminate information about AVR among them. Along with many other colleagues, he believed that Tunisian nationals' asylum applications were an "abuse of the system".

These reactions show that return counsellors constantly anticipate procedural outcomes and make guesses about the likelihood of positive decisions. Their anticipations and guesses are mainly informed by State Secretariat for Migration (SEM) statistics on asylum seekers' acceptance rates broken down by country of origin: Tunisian asylum seekers rank at the bottom. Their anticipations and guesses are further fuelled by a wide variety of notions and prejudices, some based on individual experience, that circulate among the return counsellors. Considered in this light, processing Tunisian asylum seekers' applications step by step from beginning to end is a waste of time. This delegitimisation of Tunisian applications prepares the groundwork for calls for more efficient procedures. The focus shifts away from a thorough examination of every asylum application, scrupulously following the prescribed bureaucratic path step by step, and towards reducing costs and improving the efficiency of the migration bureaucracy.

This shift accompanied the proliferation of "audit culture" (Shore and Wright 1999; 2015) in public service, which turned the main focus of state bureaucracies away from fair procedures and equal treatment and towards efficiency and cost reduction (see Hibou 2012: 46-51). AVR is a result of this shift. Yet migration bureaucracy can speed up procedure and skip certain administrative steps only with the cooperation of the potential returnees. Only an asylum seeker can renounce their legal rights to a thorough examination of their case and potential appeal of a negative decision by voluntarily revoking their asylum application. Hence, it is of the utmost importance for the success of AVR that return counsellors and potential returnees reach mutual consent, as will be explored in more detail in the next section.

In contradiction to Weber (1999: 157-234), the return migration bureaucracy shows that rule-orientation is not necessarily the basis for an ever more efficient bureaucracy. These two principles may even stand in opposition to each other. AVR is the attempt to reconcile the two conflicting principles of rule-orientation and efficiency and resolve this contradiction. It curtails asylum procedures without breaching rules. Therefore, terms such as "dignity" and "informed consent" – the latter explicitly expressed in a signed declaration-of-consent document, a pre-condition for AVR – serve to legitimise this non-compliance with strict bureaucratic rule-orientation.

Enforcing decisions "the human way" versus rule orientation

The two informants in the introductory interview referred to a further principle that stands in tension with strict rule-orientation. As the return counsellors mentioned, return migration enforcement should be executed in "a human way". Both emphasised in conversation that not a single person in the migration office would prefer forced deportation over so-called voluntary return – and not only for reasons of cost-efficiency. In AVR, one can observe that the humanitarian argument dominates other self-legitimisation strategies. This finds several different forms of expression. In addition to the above-mentioned argument that negative decisions should be enforced in "a human way", the phrase "return in dignity" is frequently deployed, an expression that is particularly common in the language of the IOM.[15] But why are return migration bureaucrats inclined to defend AVR by mobilising humanitarian arguments rather than referring to cost-efficiency

---

15 See the IOM description of assisted voluntary return and reintegration: https://www.iom.int/assisted-voluntary-return-and-reintegration [accessed 12 January 2017].

or other criteria? A simplistic answer would point out that the humanitarian argument is nothing more than a poor cover-up for a cost-benefit calculation. Forced deportation is expensive and may include pre-deportation detention, accompanied flights or even chartered special flights. Furthermore, depending on the country of origin, the success of forced deportation is highly uncertain (see Rosenberger and Küffer 2016).[16] Yet this does not answer the question of why the humanitarian argument is considered more legitimate than the cost-efficiency argument in this particular field of bureaucracy.

The majority of return migration bureaucrats whom I interviewed sincerely care that migrants have the opportunity to return "in dignity" to their country of origin, as one of them put it, echoing the IOM's official language. For her, "in dignity" means two different things. On the one hand, she associates this term with voluntariness. The return decision should be of the returnee's free will. And she considered it even more important that returnees be able to frame their return as a success and not a failure. A closer look at the self-legitimisation strategy of this particular return counsellor further illustrates this point. She is the head of a cantonal AVR office. Unlike in the first case, this AVR office is not part of the Aliens Police (*Fremdenpolizei*), which is located far away in a different part of town. Instead it belongs to the canton's welfare department. This results in a different notion of the office, a different professional ethos and a different idea of the relationship between civil servants and the public. The rule-enforcing aspect is less apparent, and return counsellors consider themselves more as service providers. When I asked this return counsellor to describe her own role, she replied:

> Look, my task is precisely not to enforce asylum decisions. My mission as a professional social worker is to assist my clients in the realisation of their decisions. If they decide to return: Fine, I will help them. If they have other plans: Fair enough. I will do what I can. But in that case, my options are limited, as you can imagine.[17]

---

16 For example, asylum seekers and migration bureaucrats are both well aware that Algeria does not accept forced deportations of its citizens. It only takes back those who return voluntarily.
17 Interview with a return migration officer, August 2014.

This informant described her role in substantially different terms from those of the two return migration bureaucrats we encountered earlier. In her self-representation, the focus is less on the enforcement of rules and decisions, and more on the relationship between the return counsellor and the asylum seekers subjected to the migration bureaucracy. She emphasised her professional ethos as a social worker who is committed to her clients as well as to the office. She regarded the double vocation towards the state and the individual migrants as part of the duty of the office, and not as a breach or weakening of bureaucratic principles. Therefore, she considered herself less as an administrator, and more as a mediator between the constraints of the migration bureaucracy and migrants' aspirations. Commitment towards the asylum seekers and a desire to take their aspirations seriously are entwined in her professional ethos. She emphasises this orientation through her frequent use of the word "client". This standpoint is different from that of the two return counsellors in the initial example who continuously use the term "asylum seeker". At the same time, "client" not only implies a more equal relationship, it also tends to conceal the structural power asymmetry at work. The term suggests that enforcement of previously made decisions stands on the same level as migrants' plans for their future. Emphasising consultation and help as the AVR's two dominant ideas, the return counsellor described her own role as though the return migration bureaucracy had temporarily suspended the dominant rule-following principle. Only by disregarding the overall logics in which return migration bureaucracy is embedded is it possible to take this stance.

In defining humanitarian reason, Didier Fassin (2012) describes how the language of compassion and suffering has replaced terms of interest, rights or justice. One can no longer address claims of the state in the antagonistic language of rights and legal entitlements, but only in the submissive mode of compassion. In the context of migration, this means that asylum has become less and less a legal entitlement, and more an act of benevolent charity in the face of unbearable suffering. AVR advances this tendency to remove rights from the forefront, as it contributes to replacing a rights-based language with the language of care. The return counsellor's statement points exactly in this direction. In mobilising a language of empowerment ("[I] assist my clients in the realisation of their decisions") she omits any reference to rights.

Conclusion: policing the boundaries of the commonwealth

Thus far, this text has examined three aspects that dominate AVR bureaucrats' self-representation: rule-orientation, striving for efficiency and humanitarian reason. The discussion of the ethnographic material has shown that none of these aspects can be reduced to procedures – i.e. to bureaucratic ethos or to bureaucratic ethics alone. The rule-following principle guarantees certainty and predictability. Efficiency can tame excessive rule-orientation and aim for fast, lean procedures. And the principle of humanitarian reason attempts to reconcile the other two bureaucratic principles that are predominantly geared towards the public good with the needs, aspirations and wishes of individual asylum seekers subjected to the migration bureaucracy.

AVR's mediation between common interests and individual claims leads us back to the boundaries of the commonwealth, and the structural incommensurability between bureaucracy's universal promises and governance of those boundaries. I have argued that bureaucracies are geared towards administration of the common good: The primary bureaucratic concern is modes of fair and just allocation of goods and services within the commonwealth, hence one benefits, at least hypothetically, from this administration of the common good in virtue of one's individual status as a member of the commonwealth. This is true even where a given bureaucratic measure is to one's individual detriment. Migration bureaucracies – and AVR in particular – primarily deal with a different issue: They distinguish those who are part of the commonwealth from those who are excluded from it. The targets of this bureaucratic administration are not included into the utopian social order; they are removed from it. The benefits AVR provides are a substitute for the bureaucratic promise of the commonwealth, from which asylum seekers are excluded.

This results in a particular relationship between the return migration bureaucracy and the people subject to its attention. Tunisian asylum seekers' migration strategies and their asylum applications can be read as a call for inclusion in the commonwealth's utopian social order: a social order from which they are excluded and which the return migration bureaucracy protects.[18] At the same time, they are affected most directly by these bureaucratic

---

18 This argument has been put forward by the thesis of the autonomy of migration (Papadopoulos et al. 2008; de Genova 2010). It appears in a different form and a context other than

interventions. Migration bureaucracy is structurally unable to incorporate these *harragas* into the utopian social order because it would imply redrawing the commonwealth's boundaries, a power that belongs to the political realm, not to the bureaucratic realm. Tunisian *harragas* call for inclusion through their sheer presence in a confrontation of "the logic of equality with the logic of the police order" (Rancière 1999: 101). The only two options in this Rancièrian political moment are repression and compassion. This structural inability of the migration bureaucracy to redraw commonwealth boundaries illustrates the aporia of universalism inscribed in bureaucratic ethics. The struggle for inclusion in the realm of the universal is always fought for and realised by those who are excluded from it (see Buck-Morss 2009). As discussion of the self-representation narratives showed, return migration bureaucrats must navigate these mutually exclusive claims. The wish to assist Tunisian asylum seekers in realising their own plans for the future collides with the exclusionary logic of the migration bureaucracy, which removes them from the commonwealth it is charged with protecting.

Bibliography

Andersson, Ruben. 2014. *Illegality, Inc: Clandestine Migration and the Business of Bordering Europe*. Berkeley: University of California Press.

Arendt, Hannah. 1986. *Elemente und Ursprünge totaler Herrschaft*. München, Zürich: Piper.

Arendt, Hannah. 1995. *Eichmann in Jerusalem: ein Bericht von der Banalität des Bösen*. 9. Aufl. Serie Piper, München: Piper.

Balibar, Étienne. 2014. *Equaliberty: Political Essays*. A John Hope Franklin Center book, Durham: Duke University Press.

Bauman, Zygmunt. 1989. *Modernity and the Holocaust*. Cambridge: Polity Press.

Bear, Laura, and Nayanika Mathur. 2015. Introduction. Remaking the Public Good: A New Anthropology of Bureaucracy. *Cambridge Anthropology* 33(1): 18–34.

---

migration and transnational mobility in James Scott's notion of the weapons of the weak (1985), where disregarding official rules is interpreted as a form of everyday rebellion.

Bayertz, Kurt. 1995. Eine kurze Geschichte der Herkunft der Verantwortung. In Kurt Bayertz, ed., *Verantwortung: Prinzip oder Problem?*, Darmstadt: Wissenschaftliche Buchgesellschaft: 3–71.

Black, Richard, and Saskia Gent. 2006. Sustainable Return in Post-Conflict Contexts. *International Migration* 44(3): 15–38.

Black, Richard, Michael Collyer and Will Sommerville. 2011. *Pay-to-Go Schemes and Other Noncoercive Return Programs: Is Scale Possible?* Washington, DC: Migration Policy Institute.

Blitz, Brad K, Rosemary Sales, and Lisa Marzano. 2005. Non-Voluntary Return? The Politics of Return to Afghanistan. *Political Studies* 53(1): 182–200.

Broeders, Dennis. 2010. Return to Sender? *Punishment & Society* 12(2): 169–186.

Buck-Morss, Susan. 2009. *Hegel, Haiti, and Universal History*. Illuminations, Pittsburgh: University of Pittsburgh Press.

Cabot, Heath. 2014. *On the Doorstep of Europe: Asylum and Citizenship in Greece.* Philadelphia: University of Pennsylvania Press.

Castañeda, Heide. 2010. Deportation Deferred. "Illegality", Visibility, and Recognition in Contemporary Germany. In: De Genova, Nicholas, and Nathalie Peutz, eds, *The Deportation Regime. Sovereignty, Space, and the Freedom of Movement.* Durham, London: Duke University Press.

De Genova, Nicholas. 2010. The Deportation Regime. Sovereignty, Space, and the Freedom of Movement. In: De Genova, Nicholas, and Nathalie Peutz, eds, *The Deportation Regime. Sovereignty, Space, and the Freedom of Movement*. Durham, London: Duke University Press: 33–65.

De Haas, Hein. 2010. Migration and Development: A Theoretical Perspective. *International Migration Review* 44 (1): 227–64.

du Gay, Paul. 2000. *In Praise of Bureaucracy: Weber, Organization and Ethics.* London: Sage Publications.

Eule, Tobias G. 2014. *Inside Immigration Law: Migration Management and Policy Application in Germany.* Ashgate Publishing.

Eule, Tobias G., David Loher and Anna Wyss. 2018. Contested Control at the Margins of the State. *Journal of Ethnic and Migration Studies* (16) 1: 2717–2729.

Fassin, Didier. 2012. *Humanitarian Reason: A Moral History of the Present.* Berkeley: University of California Press.

Ferguson, James. 2015. *Give a Man a Fish: Reflections on the New Politics of Distribution*. The Lewis Henry Morgan lectures, Durham: Duke University Press.

Geiger, Martin, and Antoine Pécoud. 2010. The Politics of International Migration Management. In Martin Geiger and Antoine Pécoud, eds, *The Politics of International Migration Management*. Houndmills, Basingstoke, Hampshire, New York: Palgrave Macmillan: 1-20.

Gosh, Bimal, ed. 2000. *Return Migration: Journey of Hope or Despair?* Geneva: International Organization for Migration IOM.

Habermas, Jürgen. 1988. *Der philosophische Diskurs der Moderne: Zwölf Vorlesungen*. 12th ed. Frankfurt am Main: Suhrkamp Verlag.

Hammond, Laura. 1999. Examining the Discourse of Repatriation: Towards a More Proactive Theory of Return Migration. In: Black, Richard, and Khalid Koser, eds, *The End of the Refugee Cycle? Refugee Repatriation and Reconstruction*. New York: Berghahn Books: 227–244.

Handelman, Don. 2004. *Nationalism and the Israeli State: Bureaucratic Logic in Public Events*. Oxford, UK, New York, NY: Berg.

Herzfeld, Michael. 1993. *The Social Production of Indifference*. University of Chicago Press.

Hoag, Colin. 2010. The Magic of the Populace: An Ethnography of Illegibility in the South African Immigration Bureaucracy. *Political and Legal Anthropology Review* 33(1): 6–25.

Horkheimer, Max. 1947. *Eclipse of Reason*. New York: Oxford University Press.

Hibou, Béatrice. 2012. *La bureaucratisation du monde à l'ère néolibérale*. Cahiers libres, Paris: La Découverte.

International Organization for Migration, ed. 2004 *Return Migration: Policies and Practices in Europe*. Geneva: International Organization for Migration.

Jazayery, Leila. 2002. The Migration-Development Nexus: Afghanistan Case Study. *International Migration* 40(5): 231–254.

Kaser, Eric and Saskia Schenker. 2008. Rückkehrhilfe der Schweiz: Bilanz und Perspektiven. *Schweizerisches Jahrbuch für Entwicklungspolitik* (27) 2: 207–220.

Lentz, Carola. 2014. "I Take an Oath to the State, not the Government": Career Trajectories and Professional Ethics of Ghanaian Public Servants. In Bierschenk, Thomas, and Jean-Pierre Olivier de Sardan, eds, *States at*

Work: Dynamics of African Bureaucracies. Africa-Europe Group for Interdisciplinary Studies, Volume 12. Leiden, Boston: Brill: 175–204.

Lietaert, Ine, Eric Broekaert and Ilse Derluyn. 2016. From Social Instrument to Migration Management Tool: Assisted Voluntary Return Programmes – The case of Belgium. *Social Policy & Administration*, (51) 7: 961-980.

Lipsky, Michael. 1980. Street-Level Bureaucracy: Dilemmas of the Individual in Public Services. New York: Russell Sage Foundation.

Moore, Sally Falk. 1972. Legal Liabilities and Evolutionary Interpretation: Some Aspects of Strict Liability, Self-Help, and Collective Responsibility. In Max Gluckman, ed., *The Allocation of Responsibility*. Manchester: Manchester University Press: 51–108.

Nelson, William. 1980. The Very Idea of Pure Procedural Justice. *Ethics* 90(4): 502–511.

Papadopoulos, Dimitris, Niamh Stephenson and Vassilis Tsianos. 2008. *Escape Routes: Control and Subversion in the Twenty-First Century*. London, Ann Arbor, MI: Pluto Press.

Rancière, Jacques. 1999. *Dis-agreement: Politics and Philosophy*. Minneapolis: University of Minnesota Press.

Rawls, John. 1999. *A Theory of Justice*. Cambridge, Mass: Belknap Press of Harvard University Press.

Sassen, Saskia. 1996. *Losing Control? Sovereignty in an Age of Globalization*. Columbia University Press.

Shore, Chris. and Susan Wright. 1999. Audit Culture and Anthropology: Neo-Liberalism in British Higher Education. *The Journal of the Royal Anthropological Institute* 5(4): 557–575.

Shore, Chris. and Susan Wright. 2015. Audit Culture Revisited: Rankings, Ratings, and the Reassembling of Society." *Current Anthropology* 56 (3): 421–444.

Scott, James C. 1985. Weapons of the Weak: Everyday Forms of Peasant Resistance. New Haven, CT, London: Yale U.P.

Tuckett, Anna. 2018. *Rules, Paper, Status: Migrants and Precarious Bureaucracy in Contemporary Italy*. Stanford, CA: Stanford University Press.

Webber, Frances. 2011. How Voluntary are Voluntary Returns? *Race & Class* 52 (4): 98–107.

Weber, Max. 1992. Wissenschaft als Beruf, 1917/1919; Politik als Beruf, 1919. In Mommsen, Wolfgang J. et al. (eds), *Max-Weber-Gesamtausgabe Abt. I, Schriften und Reden*, Tübingen: J.C.B. Mohr (Paul Siebeck).

Weber, Max. 1999. Wirtschaft und Gesellschaft: die Wirtschaft und die gesellschaftlichen Ordnungen und Mächte: Nachlass. In Hanke, Edith, and Thomas Kroll, eds, *Max-Weber-Gesamtausgabe. Abt. I, Schriften und Reden*, Tübingen: J.C.B. Mohr (P. Siebeck).

Functional Inconsistencies
State Inspection of Agricultural Labour in Switzerland

Simon Affolter

It is an ironic truism of our time that a bureaucratic apparatus often produces effects that conflict with bureaucratic goals. Such "unintended outcomes" result from complex governmental procedures that can create momentum and lead to developments that deviate from the original intent. While acknowledging the endless red tape that bureaucracies seem to generate, I aim to show analytically that it is misleading to define contra-indicated results of official practice as "unanticipated consequences" (Merton 1936; Merton 1968) or "unintended outcomes" (Foucault 1991) in reference to official government goals. As De Genova appropriately stresses, this interpretation expresses "'good faith' toward the state, and its underlying belief in the law's transparency [and] does not allow for the possibility that the law may have been instrumental in generating parameters" (2002: 432). Or, as Frank De Zwart points out: "social scientists, eager to speak truth to power, should consider the possibility that those in power may know the truth, yet let bad things happen anyway because they fear worse" (2015: 295).

Analysis of "unintended" or "unanticipated" effects from the "good faith" perspective neglects the involvement of numerous actors with varying interests in the negotiating process and in the implementation of new practices. Foucault respects these complex motivations when he observes that actors respond to outcomes by calculating, capitalizing and integrating them into their future conduct (Li 2007: 287). Thus, we should not see bureaucratic practices as pursuing one well-defined, publicly articulated goal. Rather, as Shore and Wright emphasize, the process of policy building is one of negotiation by various actors and interests (Shore and Wright 2011). Thus, the final configuration of a concrete bureaucratic practice always reflects the power relations of the actors involved in the negotiation process.

To illustrate this, I refer to the concept of hegemony projects, developed by the "Staatsprojekt Europa" research group (2012; 2014) and based on Nicos Poulantzas' neo-Gramscian approach (Poulantzas 2002). Under this view, social debates over hegemony can be structurally analysed by identifying contrasting hegemony projects, which are understood as strategic, socio-structurally framed actor-constellations that fight for interpretational sovereignty (Forschungsgruppe "Staatsprojekt Europa" 2012: 13). Thus, to understand the outcome of bureaucratic practices, we have to identify the various interests and goals that lie behind bureaucratic procedures. My approach comes close to the perspective of Laura Bear and Nayanika Mathur, who argue for remaking the public good in the anthropology of bureaucracy (2015). Referring to Osella/Osella (2001) and Ferguson (2013) in liberal thought, as the opposite of freedom. But the political anthropology of southern Africa has long recognized relations of social dependence as the very foundation of polities and persons alike. Reflecting on a long regional history of dependence 'as a mode of action' allows a new perspective on certain contemporary practices that appear to what we may call 'the emancipatory liberal mind' simply as lamentable manifestations of a reactionary and retrograde yearning for paternalism and inequality. Instead, this article argues that such practices are an entirely contemporary response to the historically novel emergence of a social world where people, long understood (under both pre-capitalist and early capitalist social systems, they see bureaucracy as "an expression of a social contract between citizens and officials that aim[s] to generate a utopian order" (Bear and Mathur 2015: 18).

This leads to the question of how to research and analyse governmental practices. According to Sharma and Gupta, "Mundane bureaucratic procedures provide important clues to understanding the micropolitics of state work, how state authority and government operate in people's daily lives, and how the state comes to be imagined, encountered, and reimagined by the population" (Sharma and Gupta 2006: 11f.). It follows that governmental practice can only be examined by observing and analysing the everyday practice of state actors interacting with civil society. This approach has led to numerous anthropological studies of street-level bureaucrats (Lipsky 2010). State agents act within a set of legal rules and norms. But they also act within a specific institutional ethos (see the Introduction to this publication). We can go even further and acknowledge the individuality of different actors working in these institutions. As agents in state institutions, individuals perform their jobs "in reference to a certain professional ethos" (Fassin et al. 2015: 6), but their work is also informed by individual ideology. Opposing values, ethics and ideas of the commonweal held by different actors (institutions and individuals) can come into conflict in daily work. One therefore cannot automatically assume that final results are unintended. Various perspectives and goals need to be taken into account if one is to accurately determine why an outcome might be considered as unintended.

The neo-Gramscian hegemony projects (Forschungsgruppe "Staatsprojekt Europa" 2014) provide helpful orientation via their top-down reading of state power. From the perspective of political science, they perform a discourse analysis of the political debates within various projects as factions fight for interpretational sovereignty in society. Here, I reverse their methodological approach by using a bottom-up anthropological perspective to analyse the effects of bureaucratic practices with regard to the various actors involved and goals pursued. My questions are simple: Who finds the effects unintended? Who finds the effects attractive? How does meaning change for different actors? What measures are implemented in reaction to the results and why (or why not)? In my following empirical study of vegetable production in Switzerland's central plateau, I focus on the agents responsible for labour market inspections and use an anthropological approach to interpret the results of their efforts.

The association for labour market inspections

In 2008, the new Federal Act on Illegal Employment (*Bundesgesetz gegen die Schwarzarbeit BGSA*) came into force in Switzerland. According to the Act, "illegal employment should be combated. To do this, administrative improvements and measures concerning inspections and sanctions [have been] designed" (BGSA, Abs. 1, Art. 1). Upon its implementation, every Canton in Switzerland was directed to create an institution responsible for inspections in the labour market. This law and the regulatory institutions it established were also related to the free movement of people within Europe. To prevent transnational enterprises from systematically undermining Swiss labour standards, so-called "accompanying measures" allowed authorities to impose sanctions on employers who were not domiciled in Switzerland. Thus, the legal requirement of equal treatment was fulfilled: all working relationships in an economic sector in Switzerland were to be treated equally, independent of the employer's legal residence.

In the Swiss canton where I performed my ethnographic fieldwork,[1] an association was soon established with the task of inspecting labour conditions in various economic sectors. Associated with the canton's Office for the Economy, it now functions as a para-state institution under the leadership of government representatives and employer and employee organisations. The association's executive board consists of representatives of the canton and of joint committees[2] from various business sectors. The association has a staff of nine, including six inspectors.[3] In addition to the Act on Illegal Employment, the regulatory work of the association also involves other pieces of legislation, including the Federal Act on Measures Accompanying the Free Movement of Persons (*Flankierende Massnahmen*), the Collective Employment Contracts (*Gesamtarbeitsverträge GAV*) and the National Collective Employment Agreements (*Landesmantelverträge*) regarding employment relationships. The numerous migrant workers employed in low-wage sectors that the association is responsible for regulating mean that laws pertaining to residence and asylum also matter. Finally, as a regulatory body within the labour market, the association has the task of identifying actions necessary to improve labour conditions.

In the following, I will focus on the inspection practice of this association and the effects this has on vegetable farmers in the Swiss agricultural sector, my field of research. In my fieldwork, I observed people employed on farms, describing recruitment procedures, labour conditions and daily life. The vast majority of employees on these farms are migrants. Some of them have settlement permits, others have temporary residence permits and still others have no permission to stay or work in Switzerland at all. The regulation of migrant labour is mostly the responsibility of two government departments,

---

1 In my research, I documented numerous irregular labour contracts, whereby the labourers are mostly illegalised people in Switzerland. In my thesis, I also describe existing networks acting as informal employment agencies. Therefore, I anonymise the region of my research and all the involved actors to protect the autonomy of these people (cf. Düvell, Triandafyllidou, and Vollmer 2009).

2 "Joint Committee" is a translation of the Swiss term "Paritätische Kommission," which addresses Swiss labour rights. The Paritätische Kommission is composed of equal numbers of employers and employee representatives.

3 "Inspector" is the official term for persons who conduct control procedures.

with different areas of responsibility: The Office for Migration is responsible for granting residence permits and several kinds of work permits; the Department for Economic Affairs grants several other kinds of permits and monitors conditions in the labour market. Hence, the Association for Labour Market Inspections represents the nexus between the two governmental departments even as it represents state authority in the agricultural sector.

Since there are no collective bargaining or other obligatory agreements for wage labour in the agricultural sector, there is no joint committee of employer and employee organizations responsible for ordering inspections. It is therefore up to Canton authorities to determine an annual quota, assigning the association to investigate specific abnormalities detected in documents filed during the process of obtaining a work permit. Before a work permit can be issued, the Office for the Economy must review the employment contract to check whether it complies with labour-law provisions. Binding legal norms may exist in the form of a national collective bargaining agreement (*Gesamtarbeitsvertrag GAV*) or a standard employment contract (*Normalarbeitsvertrag NAV*) with binding minimum wages. For the agricultural sector, however, no national contract exists, only Canton NAVs without binding minimum wages. Farmers are "Swiss Employers whose activity does not fall under the scope of an average GAV or NAV with binding minimum wages and will not be sanctioned automatically if they undercut the usual wage. If the TPK [tripartite commission] discover the usual wages are being undercut, a mutual agreement procedure is conducted with the relevant employer" (SECO 2015: 27, author's translation). In mutual agreement procedures, the aim is to set an appropriate wage increase in accordance with the existing standard employment contract. The Swiss Code of Obligations provides the legal basis for this procedure (Art 360b, para. 3.):

> The commissions monitor the labour market. If they observe abusive practices within the meaning of Article 360a paragraph 1, they normally seek to reach agreement directly with the employers concerned. Where this cannot be achieved within two months, they petition the competent authority to issue a standard employment contract fixing a minimum wage for the affected sectors or occupations (SECO 2015: 27, author's translation).

Thus, the results of inspection activities can influence labour law. If institutions carrying out inspections detect standard wages regularly being undercut in a particular sector, a NAV with binding minimum wages can be issued. At the national level, this has only happened for domestic workers. The federal government's 2008 study made clear that domestic workers from low-wage countries were generally employed for wages lower than for comparable work in other sectors.[4] As a result, an NAV with binding minimum wages was drafted in 2010 and has been in force since early 2011.

In the agricultural sector, no such contract exists, nor was there ever a powerful push for one. There are several reasons for this. First of all, migrant farm workers are not represented by a powerful interest group. In Switzerland, standard wages are negotiated on a sector-by-sector basis according to the tripartite neo-corporatism model (where negotiations are held among representatives of labour unions, employers and the government). In annual negotiation processes, they define recommended wages and working hours in the agricultural sector. This non-binding NAV is mainly negotiated between the Farmers' Association and the small ABLA union that represents farm employees. I had an opportunity to talk with the union president, Paul Sommer. He explained to me that it is very hard to negotiate with other labour unions, because they "have no idea about the conditions in agriculture" and therefore would price labour out of the market. He agrees that wages should be raised in the sector, "but not in a way that is disproportionate to the conditions in agriculture". Here, he does not identify with the numerous migrant labourers in this sector, but rather places himself strongly on the side of the farmers and the problems farmers face. The reason for this became clear when he explained that his union mainly represents skilled agricultural labourers: the president himself oversees farm production at one of Switzerland's bigger prisons.

Because systematic labour inspections have never been enforced in the agricultural sector, the sector is underrepresented in discussions of statistical data. With only 243 companies and 723 workers subject to inspection nationally, agriculture has among the lowest inspection numbers of any sector (SECO 2017: 18). Thus, it is not a priority for governmental authorities, nor for regulatory associations. This lack of statistical data makes it almost impossible to identify agricultural labour conditions that do not correspond

---

4 "Le travail domestique en Suisse – Calcul d'un seuil de salaire en usage en vue de l'édition d'un contrat-type de travail au sein du secteur des Services domestiques en Suisse", Prof. Yves Flückiger, Observatoire Universitaire de l'Emploi (OUE), Université de Genève.

with the NAV. The activities of the Association for Labour Market Inspections resemble pure data collection. Because of the low number of inspections, limited capacity to undertake checks, and the lack of binding legal norms in this sector, the scope of regulatory activity is quite limited. Nevertheless, the little data that is collected is statistically evaluated and collated in the annual report on labour inspections, where it adds credence to the interpretation that labour law is well respected in practice in the agricultural sector. It follows that the agricultural sector is never the focus of labour market inspections, and no effort has been made to adopt binding contracts for agricultural labour. There is another effect: the comparatively low number of deviations from the law in the data contributes to the perception that working conditions are satisfying for agricultural employees. Therefore, the low wages and excessive working hours compared with almost every other sector are not questioned.

Labour inspections generate data that disguises precarious labour conditions and protects the agricultural sector from critical public debate. This has already influenced the outcome of a political intervention. In 2014, the Canton of Geneva applied for a regular working contract with binding minimum wages. Geneva's representatives argued that different working conditions in the cantons lead to uneven market conditions. In its answer, the Federal Council referred to the collected labour control data:

> The Tripartite Commission of the Confederation is aware of the fact that downward pressure on salaries occur and that workers from low-wage EU countries bear the brunt of this. But the volume of reported cases is not at a level that would justify the establishment of national minimum wages. [...] such a contract for fixing minimum wages can only be realised at the request of the Tripartite Commission of the Confederation. [...] Labour costs affect the prices of products, and the poor wage conditions and/or downward pressure on salaries lead to unfair competition in the agricultural market, which increases price pressure. This unacceptable situation is jeopardising farms that deliver locally produced food and create jobs. This entails the risk that a part of the local agricultural production disappears and is replaced by imports, all in all an absurd situation.[5]

---

5 https://www.parlament.ch/de/ratsbetrieb/suche-curia-vista/geschaeft?AffairId=20140308 [accessed 25 October 2016, author's translation].

As we see, the collected data constitutes an instrument to legitimate the *status quo* for farm employees. Potential improvements in labour conditions for farm workers in Switzerland are discussed in economic terms, comparing the competitiveness of national agricultural products with imported products from low-wage countries. Agricultural competitiveness rather than living wages had become the focus of the discussion.

The Association for Labour Market Inspections operated under these conditions in the Canton where I did my fieldwork. There, I talked with the chief inspector about the activities of the association and accompanied another inspector on his trips in the field.

This association was originally established under pressure from labour unions seeking to inspect labour conditions in the construction industry via an independent institution specifically designed for that purpose. Besides these activities, the institution ensured compliance with the GAVs and documented labour conditions for wider public and political usage, as the union representative in the canton explained me (interview from 20 February 2014). Chief inspector Simon Heine [name changed], who coordinated inspection activities in the association, has been on the board since its early days. At that time, Heine was already a member of the relevant labour union, having previously worked in the construction industry. In his work as an inspector, he saw an opportunity to put his labour union ideals into action and combat serious shortcomings in the construction industry.

Before the association took over inspection activities, the Canton's farmers' association had carried out the relevant inspections in the agricultural sector. For the farmers' association, this mandate meant a conflict of interests, a representative told me (interview from 18 January 2014). The farmers' association represents for the interests of farmers in their dealings with cantonal and national authorities. Thus, it is effectively an employers' organisation for the agricultural sector and unsuitable for inspecting labour conditions. The canton's farmers' association was pleased when the mandate for inspecting the labour market was handed over to an independent institution.

As Chief Inspector Heine explains, the association's workload is generally very heavy. It currently carries out some 80 inspections each year in the agricultural sector under the Canton's mandate. The chief inspector explains that agricultural operations play a special role in the labour market, and people working as association inspectors need to have an appropriate profile. People with no idea of working conditions in the agricultural sector lack sufficient understanding to undertake farm inspections and deal with the farmers. For example, on most farms working hours are not recorded. In such circumstances, one must "simply trust in the farmers" (Interview from 11 January 2014). Generally, inspectors have an adequate understanding of the circumstances, although the agricultural sector is a "tough industry". When I remarked that this is also the case in other sectors where the association is responsible for controls, Heine immediately compared it to the construction industries where he worked for years and "knows, what he is talking about". Construction work is also very tough, "this is absolutely the case". But in the agricultural sector it is difficult "to keep the farm alive". In the context of labour inspections, farmers are not perceived as employers, as are owners in other sectors of the economy. Due to difficult market conditions for agricultural products, farmers have acquired a special status. Within the association, the perception and motivation for inspections in agriculture are different from those in the construction industry, for example. In construction, Heine wants to "affect something with the controls", he wants to fight "illegal, inhuman and often mafia-like" practices.

Taking over the mandate for the agricultural sector meant an increase of the annual quota of inspections without a rise in the number of association inspectors. It is therefore necessary to prioritise among the sectors when determining where inspections should be carried out. Because there are no public reports of illegal employment and few abnormalities have been monitored by inspections, the agricultural sector is not treated as a priority. This has a strong impact on the practice of inspections in this sector, as inspectors try to reach the commissioned annual quota as efficiently as possible. Chief Inspector Heine explained to me that inspectors pay attention to the number of workers in the fields when carrying out in spontaneous checks. They tend to perform inspections on fields with many workers, not on fields with only a few people working. This practice can be seen in annual statistics: in 2016, 156 checks of people were carried out on 25 farms, corresponding to an average of 6.2 checks per farm. For smaller farms, a working group of six people is a lot. Thus, efficient practice means that the Association primarily performs inspections on larger farms.

When I accompanied an association inspector on his inspection trip in the agricultural sector, I noticed right away his obvious strategies to circumvent conflicts between personal and professional ethics. The activities he carried out while performing inspections scarcely resembled the officially communicated goals. I will discuss these inconsistencies in terms of my theoretical approach at the end of the chapter.

Inspection practice in the field

> "I imagine how the farmer must answer questions from his colleagues in the evening at the regulars' table"

Association inspector Frank Gubser (name changed) often carries out inspections in the agricultural sector. He learned carpentry after school, then switched to nursing a few years later, and finally completed an apprenticeship as a lumberman. After ten years working on reconstruction projects in Latin America, he returned to Switzerland and is now employed by the association as an inspector. The work is well suited to his philosophy of life, Frank explains. His life expectancy is over 80 years, and his time should be filled up usefully with social engagement. In his opinion, too much stress is placed on the role of the individual these days. He may not revolutionise the labour market with his work, but he can uncover cases of abuse, and thus contribute to the improvement of working conditions.

On the day I accompanied him, Gubser brought along two portfolios with work permits for farms he wanted to inspect. In one case a young French woman is working on a horse farm for a gross wage of 2,200 Swiss Francs per month (about the same in US dollars at 2019 exchange rates).[6] Frank calls this a "bourgeois" case. The employer is abusing the dreams of a young woman who loves to work with horses and would do anything for that opportunity. The second case is a farm that grows berries. The farmer applied for five work permits, a "highly unlikely" number for berry harvesting. Berries are extremely labour-intensive and the harvest "cannot be managed with only five employees". In addition to these two cases, Gubser also planned to perform a number of spontaneous inspections that day.

First we visit the berry farm. Inspector Gubser looks at the berry fields next to the farmer's house as we driving by. We cannot see anyone working

---

6 The NAV stipulates a gross monthly wage of 3,200 Swiss Francs. This is still 1,000 Swiss Francs lower than the wage for an unskilled worker in the building industry.

on these fields. Then, we drive directly to the farm and park in the backyard, where the farmer's wife immediately welcomes us. Our identification as association inspectors makes her a little nervous, she explains, because the timing of the inspection is extremely unfavourable since there is a lot of work to do. Frank asks the woman about the berry fields: how is it possible to harvest the berries with only five employees? The woman replies that their customers pick the berries themselves. For Gubser, this explanation is satisfactory and the two talk about how self-picking can benefit a farmer's operation. Then Frank asks where the employees are working at the moment. The woman refers us to an older Polish employee who was just driving off in a small van. After briefly consulting with the farmer's wife, he leads us to the "lower field". Other people were also working "up the hill", but that field was not easily accessible by car. After a short drive we arrive with Jacek (name changed) at an asparagus field. Five employees are planting new seedlings. The "group leader" calls the employees together and explains what the inspection is for. He is the only one of the foreign workers to understand some German. All the employees carry copies of their passports, which is why the procedure is completed rapidly. All the names are recognised by the system and each worker has a short-term residence permit. Finally, Gubser asks the group leader about working conditions on the farm. He asks suggestive questions, such as "Did the farmer organise an apartment for you on the farm? How many hours do you work per week, 52?" and so on. All suggestions are affirmed by the group leader without exception. After this control procedure, we talk a little about planting asparagus and the harvest. Then we leave these people and drive on.

This example shows what Simon Heine indicated in my first conversation: It is important to trust the farmers when performing control procedures in agricultural sectors. In this example we were deliberately piloted to a specific field to question the workers there. Whether the people working on the other field "up the hill" all had residence and work permits was not known. Nor were the original concerns that led to this farm being inspected followed up, even though Frank Gubser is absolutely aware of them. But "complete verification of a company is just simply impossible in the course of my work", as he told me after this visit. Otherwise, only one operation could be conducted in a working day. Thus, the quality of inspections is subordinate to the quantity of inspections conducted per day. This is not surprising. The heavy association workload and performance agreements with the Canton define the number of inspections per year.

Next, Gubser wants to visit the "bourgeois case". Again we study the case documents. The employment contract for the French woman indeed notes a gross wage of CHF 2,200. Frank explains to me that this is a classic case: employers often mix up the kind of employment contract that should be given to the normal work force with those that apply to au pairs. The inspector defines "hybrid contracts" of the kinds often given to au pairs as problematic. They set improper standards in the labour market and therefore offer false incentives. When we examine the French woman's employment contract more closely, we notice that it had expired two weeks earlier. We therefore cancel the farm visit, even though Gubser is disappointed that this case "slipped through his fingers". It is important to "make a mark" in such situations, he says, because such cases have barely and consequences for the employer, according to the law. The problem is that most employment relationships of this kind are not considered abusive by the employees. It is remarkable that Frank does not evaluate regular employment contracts in the agricultural sector in the same manner, since working hours, wages and working conditions in general are significantly worse than in every other sector. Frank explains that he absolutely lacks the time to perform inspection activities satisfactorily in the agricultural sector. This was why the current case had been lying on his desk for a long time. Throughout the previous few weeks, he had been totally absorbed in a large construction site.

In the afternoon, Gubser shows me the procedure for a spontaneous inspection in the fields, what he calls a "field inspection". We are driving on a country road when we see two workers weeding in a field. Frank stops the car and explains to them that we are inspectors from the Association for Labour Market Inspections. Both workers come from Poland and do not speak any German. Since one of them is working his third season on that farm, he finally understands what he has to do. He explains what is happening to his colleague and together we drive to the farmer's house – the two Polish workers on the tractor in front and Frank and I following in the car. When we arrive at the farm, we are friendly. Although he is a little frightened and scared, the farmer welcomes us. Frank explains that it is only a standard check of work permits for his employees and that nothing has happened. The farmer then calls his wife out of the house. As the farm's business manager, she brings the required documents in a ring binder. The inspection of the two workers' documents is quickly performed: both have work permits for six months. The farmer tells us that he finds it very important that such checks are performed. Otherwise in the village, many farmers would have been employing people illegally. He would never do that, but he might be an exception. Many of his colleagues would not care about the law, they would just search for cheap labour. This leads to a discussion between the inspector and the farmer about the negative effects of illegal employment for both employees and employers. Both men have the same opinion about illegal employment, share anecdotes and discuss consequences. After a warm goodbye we drive off.

Back in the car, I ask Frank Gubser about his experiences with "field inspections" in the past. Having seen no abnormalities in this control, I ask about situations where irregularities were noted. Frank enters a narrative mode. His stories are exciting and a motivating aspect of his job. The most tragic situation he encountered during his controls was on a small farm with a restaurant on the premises. There, a woman from Mongolia had been working for five years. The woman milked the cows in the morning, then prepared meals for the restaurant and did domestic work as well. She was regularly raped by the farmer and sometimes even by his son, when he visited. Frank is very involved in this story. This situation shows what can happen if a female worker is not protected by labour laws, Frank tells me. This leads me to ask about the consequences of this shocking story, and about the involvement of inspectors in procedures following inspections. Gubser sees this as a problem. According to formal process, inspectors are completely excluded from procedures following inspections and receive no information about them. But Frank Gubser has an extensive network of contacts among the institutions that prosecute cases arising from inspections, and can always inform himself about cases where he was the in-field inspector. In the case of the Mongolian woman, the procedural results were very double-edged, as Frank calls it. Because she was in Switzerland illegally, the woman was deported despite her tragic story. Here, the limits of his work come very clearly to light. Although it is critical that abuses be uncovered, his working relationship ends with discovery. Penalties for malefactors are not always satisfactory: for the Mongolian woman, this was definitely true.

How Gubser assessed this and other cases leads to the question of what can be called a "good inspection activity". Frank has a clear answer and explains it to me in reference to another case. Two years earlier, he wanted to carry out checks on two workers in a field. But when he stopped his car and opened the door, the two men dropped everything and ran off. He was happy to let them run. The reason was clear to him: they had no work permits and very likely no residence permits. He documented the situation by photographing the full and empty vegetable crates, tools and other traces of activity. This is important, he explains, because he needed exhibits for the report. Otherwise, one could simply deny that the two men had been working in the field. Although it was late, he called the police requesting immediate assistance because the two men had fled. He wanted to make a "real spectacle" out of it with "police cars, sirens and uniforms". Frank loved imagining "how the farmer must [have] answer[ed] questions by his colleagues in the evening at the regulars' table"[7] about the incident. Something like that has an effect, Frank thinks. The two underprivileged men were not punished because of their illegal status. Frank's personal goal was not to detect illegal workers. The aliens law is not as important to Frank as working conditions and employers who abuse employees. These are what he wants to detect in his work. When telling this story, Frank smiles: "This is the ideal situation for me".

From "unintended consequences" to questions of power

As we can see, governmental labour inspection practice in my field of research is characterised by various inconsistencies. But inconsistency does not make a bureaucratic practice dysfunctional. From an administrative standpoint, the inspection procedure works well. The proposed number of checks can be achieved satisfactorily, the data collected is relevant and can be analysed. But this practice does nothing to improve labour conditions in the agricultural sector nor to represented them accurately for political and public debate. Instead, it supports the interpretation of labour law as "highly respected", and validates the perception that agricultural work carried out under regular work contracts is "fair". This can be explained using Handelmans' important analysis of bureaucracy as fundamentally built on categories (Handelman 2004). Compared with other categories, the category of legal working conditions appears to be the best, and "fairest" option. Except

---

7 The "regulars' table" (*Stammtisch*) denote a specific table in a restaurant which is reserved for regular guests. Often, the table is frequented by different groups of people during the day. In the evening, it is the place to meet friends after work. In general, it is a man's place.

for wages, contract compliance is not the main focus of the inspections, and inspection practice is limited to examining residence and work permits.

Labour inspections in the field pursue various interests and goals. Federal authorities have the overarching goal of combatting informal work, because undeclared work contributes to the loss of public funds. At the same time, inspections are supposed to be a means of improving labour conditions. This is apparent in Frank's practice in the field and in his understanding of his work. Professional morals and personal morals are almost entirely congruent (Fassin 2015). But the goals and interests of various groups also shape inspection practice and interpretations of the resulting data.

The belief that agriculture is a "hard business" is ubiquitous: this interpretation is applied not just to the work of employees, but alto to the practice of agriculture itself. Farmers are not seen as employers and managers, because they are still highly involved in the labour process. Furthermore, the ongoing transformation of the agricultural sector towards larger, more industrialised farms jeopardises smaller family farms. For these reasons, there is widespread acceptance that sanctions should not be existential. A certain tolerance should be encouraged even if it is inconsistent with labour law. This hegemonic perspective is deeply rooted and contributes to political debates.

Agriculture has a unique position in the political landscape of Switzerland. To ensure food security for the national population, production is highly subsidised by the state (Tanner 1992; Moser 2011). As part of the global food regime, however, agricultural production endures permanent competition with imports from low-wage countries (McMichael 2013). Therefore, precarious labour conditions are officially acknowledged as a precondition for competitive and sustainable national farms. This interpretation also influences labour's engagement with farm work. None of the powerful labour unions is active in the agricultural sector, although the small, specialised ABLA union negotiates regular working contracts with the farmers' association. As I have shown, this union shares the perception that agriculture cannot be compared with other economic sectors. What we thus see is a neo-corporatist model of labour union engagement, reflecting a hegemonic view of the place of agricultural work within society and the economy (Jessop 2015). In this process, no substantive representation exists for unskilled, seasonal employees, most of whom are migrants.

In a further interpretation of inspection practices formulated by a different state actor, an agent from the Office of Migration told me in an interview that labour market inspections can also be used to detect illegal residents. Labour inspection practice thus becomes a means of residency control, as it identifies people living and working without permits on state territory. But, as already shown, association inspectors circumvent this function when it conflicts with the individual morality and ideology of professional action.

Describing these effects as unintended is thus misleading, rather it becomes a question of integrating the perspectives and manifold interests of various actors. Some inspectors develop strategies to diminish the effects of their work that clash with their personal ethics. Nationally, agricultural inspection procedure seems to have "unintended" (in terms of *unwanted*) effects regarding the improvement of labour conditions. The Federal Council statement on the political initiative to define binding minimum wages (cited above) shows that collected data from agricultural labour inspections effected just the opposite: it was used to justify non-intervention in the labour-law provisions of the agricultural sector.

But this unintended and unwelcome outcome for agricultural workers becomes an attractive outcome if we shift perspective. As I have written elsewhere, the data collected by the inspection practice is not representative of the highly hierarchical and ethnicised labour market in the sector (Affolter 2013; Bopp and Affolter 2013). Generally, precarious working conditions ensure cheap production. Because of intensive national and international price pressure on fresh fruit and vegetable markets, cheap production is a precondition for economic success. The farmers integrate workers with irregular working contracts into their personnel by engaging (illegalised) people in labour intensive phases during the harvest season. But in doing this, they pursue the strategy of not letting these people work with those employed on regular contracts in the fields. Irregularly engaged workers mostly work separated on secluded fields to prevent checks by inspectors or the police. This strategy, together with the protectionist agenda of numerous political actors, including the farmers' association, is what James C. Scott calls the art of not being governed (2009). This is why it is vital to stress who it is that reaps the economic benefits of low-wage work when analysing production relations in a given sector. Rather than dismissing the effects presented here as "unintended," I highlight and analyse the inconsistency of this bureaucratic practice. Different ideals of the public good and formal goals of bureaucratic practices may converge in such a way that the hierarchy of goals and laws becomes obvious: the goal of decent labour conditions contravenes the wider economic goal of protecting the Swiss agricultural sector.

This leads us back to my original question about intention and bureaucratic practice. When the effects of bureaucratic practice do not correspond with officially declared goals, we should not immediately assume this is unintended. First we need to ask: Who finds the effects unintended? Who finds the effects attractive? How does meaning change for different actors? What measures are implemented in reaction to the results and why (or why not)? Here, the bureaucratic procedure followed by agricultural labour inspectors produces statistical data that is used to protect the status quo of agricultural production in Switzerland, and to discourage public and political interventions to improve labour law in the sector. Better working conditions with higher wages and fewer working hours would challenge the value chain of agricultural production. This shows that bureaucratic procedures have functional outcomes often determined more by ad hoc assumptions and agreements than by written law. Anthropological analysis from the bottom up gives us insights about hegemonies inherent in negotiation processes that determine state practices. State tolerance of precarious work (by mainly non-citizens) in the agricultural sector does not reflect bureaucratic ineptitude, but rather represents prioritisation of economic aspects of national agricultural production. This prioritisation of economic interests, in combination with migrant workers' lack of political representation, guarantees cheap production costs and contributes to the continuing precariousness of these workers' working and living conditions.

Bibliography

Affolter, Simon. 2013. Moderne Knechte Und Mägde. *Terra Cognita*, no. 22: 40–42.
Bear, Laura, and Nayanika Mathur. 2015. Introduction. *The Cambridge Journal of Anthropology* 33 (1): 18–34.
Bopp, Tina, and Simon Affolter. 2013. Vom helvetischen Flüchtling bis zur neukolonialen Knechtschaft in der Landwirtschaft. In Ruth Gurny and Ueli Tecklenburg, eds, *Arbeit ohne Knechtschaft: Bestandesaufnahme und Forderungen rund um das Thema Arbeit*, 94–111. Denknetz-Buch. Zürich: Edition 8.

De Genova, Nicholas. 2002. Migrant "Illegality" and Deportability in Everyday Life. *Annual Review of Anthropology* 31: 419–47.

De Zwart, Frank. 2015. Unintended But Not Unanticipated Consequences. *Theory and Society* 44 (3): 283–97.

Düvell, Franck, Anna Triandafyllidou and Bastian Vollmer. 2009. Ethical Issues in Irregular Migration Research in Europe. *Population, Space and Place* 16 (January): 227–39. https://doi.org/10.1002/psp.590.

Fassin, Didier. 2015. Maintaining Order. The Moral Justification for Police Practices. In Didier Fassin et al., eds, *At the Heart of the State: The Moral World of Institutions*, edited by. Anthropology, Culture and Society. London: Pluto Press: 93–116.

Fassin, Didier, et al. 2015. *At the Heart of the State: The Moral World of Institutions*. Anthropology, Culture and Society. London: Pluto Press.

Ferguson, James. 2013. Declarations of Dependence: Labour, Personhood, and Welfare in Southern Africa. *Journal of the Royal Anthropological Institute* 19 (2): 223–42.

Forschungsgruppe 'Staatsprojekt Europa', ed., 2012. *Die EU in Der Krise: Zwischen Autoritärem Etatismus Und Europäischem Frühling.* Verlag Westfälisches Dampfboot.

———. 2014. *Kämpfe Um Migrationspolitik: Theorie, Methode Und Analysen Kritischer Europaforschung.* Kultur Und Soziale Praxis. Bielefeld: transcript.

Foucault, Michel. 1991. *Discipline and Punish: The Birth of the Prison.* London: Penguin Books.

Handelman, Don. 2004. *Nationalism and the Israeli State: Bureaucratic Logic in Public Events.* Oxford: Berg.

Jessop, Bob. 2015. Corporatism and Beyond? On Governance and Its Limits. In Eva Hartmann and Poul F. Kjaer, eds, *The Evolution of Intermediary Institutions in Europe.* Palgrave Macmillan UK: 29–46.

Li, Tania Murray. 2007. *The Will to Improve: Governmentality, Development, and the Practice of Politics.* Durham: Duke University Press.

Lipsky, Michael. 2010. *Street-Level Bureaucracy: Dilemmas of the Individual in Public Services.* 30th anniversary expanded edition. New York: Russell Sage Foundation.

McMichael, Philip. 2013. *Food Regimes and Agrarian Questions.* Halifax: Fernwood Books.

Merton, Robert K. 1936. The Unanticipated Consequences of Purposive Social Action. *American Sociological Review* 1 (6): 894–904.

———. 1968. *Social Theory and Social Structure*. 1968 enlarged ed edition. New York: The Free Press.

Moser, Peter. 2011. Von der "organischen" zur "industriellen" Agrarmodernisierung. In Peter Martig, Heinrich Christoph Affolter and Charlotte Gutscher, eds, *Berns Moderne Zeit: Das 19. Und 20. Jahrhundert neu entdeckt*. Berner Zeiten. Bern: Stämpfli Verlag: 287–91.

Osella, Caroline, and Filippo Osella. 2001. The Return of King Mahabali: The Politics of Morality in South India. In Christopher John Fuller, ed, *The Everyday State and Society in Modern India*, 137–62. London: Hurst & Company.

Poulantzas, Nicos. 2002. *Staatstheorie: Politischer Überbau, Ideologie, Autoritärer Etatismus*. Hamburg: VSA.

Scott, James C. 2009. *The Art of Not Being Governed: An Anarchist History of Upland Southeast Asia*. New Haven: Yale University Press.

SECO, Staatssekretariat für Wirtschaft. 2015. *Umsetzung Der Flankierenden Massnahmen Zum Freien Personenverkehr Schweiz – EU Im Jahre 2014*. https://biblio.parlament.ch/e-docs/381279.pdf.

———. 2017. *BERICHT Vollzug Des Bundesgesetzes Über Massnahmen Zur Bekämpfung Der Schwarzarbeit 1. Januar 2016 Bis 31. Dezember 2016*. https://www.seco.admin.ch/dam/seco/de/dokumente/Publikationen_Dienstleistungen/Publikationen_Formulare/Arbeit/Personenfreizuegigkeit_Arbeitsbeziehungen/Studien%20und%20Berichte/Berichte_massnahmen_bekaempfung_schwarzarbeit/BGSA-Bericht_2016.pdf.download.pdf/BGSA-Bericht_2016.pdf.

Sharma, Aradhana, and Akhil Gupta, eds, 2006. *The Anthropology of the State: A Reader*. 1 edition. Malden, MA; Oxford: Wiley-Blackwell.

Shore, Cris, and Susan Wright. 2011. Introduction. Conseptualisung Policy: Technologies of Governance and the Politics of Visibility. In Davide Però, Cris Shore and Susan Wright, eds, *Policy Worlds: Anthropology and the Analysis of Contemporary Power*. Yew York: Berghahn: 1–25.

Tanner, Albert. 1992. Einleitung: Die Bauern in der Schweizer Geschichte. In Albert Tanner and Anne-Lise Head-König, eds, *Die Bauern in der Geschichte der Schweiz: Les Paysans dans l'histoire de la Suisse*. Schweizerische Gesellschaft für Wirtschafts- und Sozialgeschichte 10 (10). Zürich: Chronos.

The Economy of Detainability
Theorizing Migrant Detention

Nicholas De Genova[1]

The dramatic expansion in recent years of an effectively global deportation regime (De Genova and Peutz 2010) – and the accompanying widening purview of deportability for migrants, which has been the effect of diversified and intensified forms of "interior" immigration law enforcement – has generated the conditions of possibility for an analogous expansion of migrant detention. In this article, I offer the beginnings of a conception of migrant detention in terms of an economy of detainability and the wider disciplinary ramifications of this condition of susceptibility to detention as an amalgam of the deprivation of liberty, spatial confinement, temporal interruption and indeterminacy. Notably, it is not the principal task of this essay to elaborate any specific ethnographic or historical example, as such. Rather, the primary concerns here are theoretical and critical. It is remarkable that the general dynamics that I will sketch here are in no sense confined to the ethnographic particulars or socio-historical peculiarities of any specific (nation-)state or its legal regime, or the specific ethics or ethos of any particular immigration bureaucracy (see, e.g. Welch and Schuster 2005). This fact could arguably be taken to suggest that – at least with regard to the detention and deportation of illegalized migrants – we have been witnessing a significant harmonization of how diverse and discrepant immigration bureaucracies and their enforcement regimes conceptualize their official roles in superintending the

---

[1] An earlier and less elaborated version of this article was published online by the Global Detention Project as "Detention, Deportation, and Waiting: Toward a Theory of Migrant Detainability," Global Detention Project, Working Paper No. 18 (1 December 2016): <https://www.globaldetentionproject.org/detention-deportation-waiting-toward-theory-migrant-detainability-gdp-working-paper-no-18>.

formal inclusions and exclusions that are taken to demarcate the parameters of the best interests of the common weal. With regard to the figure of the illegalized migrant (notably including that of the rejected "asylum-seeker"), in other words, it seems plausible that there has been an increasing consonance across the planet of the ethos of supremely rational, rule-oriented public service among immigration bureaucracies as well as their procedural ethics, as evinced by the proliferation and generalization of migrant detention and deportation. This alone commands reflection and merits critical scrutiny.

Rather than presenting a detailed empirical case study or a mass of original research findings, therefore, I want to propose some ideas that might offer a fresh critical perspective for the purpose of understanding the more global phenomenon of migrant detention. Indeed, critical reflection on migrant detention may have something significant to contribute to a more rigorous approach to both theory and practice in challenging the injustices that confront an ever widening cross-section of migrants, refugees, and others categorized as non-citizens within the immigration bureaucracies and juridical and law enforcement regimes of (nation-)states around the world. Gathering insights from a variety of geographically diverse research in numerous disciplines, then, this article is dedicated to formulating concepts that may inform how we understand what is at stake in the multifarious confrontations between immigration bureaucracies and enforcement agencies and those whom they deem to be disposable (detainable or deportable) and effectively outside of the common weal to which they presume to dedicate their energies. Put somewhat differently, this essay hopes to elucidate some of what is at stake when detention becomes a site of migrant struggles.

Deportability / Detainability

One of the defining features of the sociopolitical condition of migrants, whatever their precise juridical status within the larger immigration system of any given (nation-)state, is the susceptibility to deportation that is a virtually universal feature of their non-citizen status. Within any given regime of immigration-related conditionalities and contingencies (Goldring and Landolt 2013; cf. Chauvin and Garcés-Mascareñas 2012; Coutin 2003), migrants always remain more or less deportable. This is what we may understand to be an "economy" of *deportability*: even if all non-citizens are potentially subject to deportation, not everyone is deported, and not everyone is subject to deportation to the same degree; there is, in other words, *an unequal distribution* of the various forms of this particular power over non-citizens' lives and liberties, as well as the rationalities and techniques or technologies deployed in the administration or government of migrants' lives through recourse to the means to deport them, or to serve them deportation orders (without actually deporting them), or otherwise to refrain from deporting them or mandating their deportation. And yet, even in spite of such an uneven distribution of deportation, this condition of deportability – this possibility of being deported, of being forcibly expelled from the space where migrants are actively engaged in making their lives and livelihoods – has profoundly disciplinary repercussions (De Genova 2002; 2005:213-50; 2010b; 2014).

The widening purview of deportation over the last decade or two, on an effectively global scale, has been predictably accompanied by a comparable expansion of migrant detention.

In this article, I am indeed focused specifically on *migrant* detention. Nonetheless, from the outset, we must recognize that there is a fundamental difference between deportability and what I call *detainability* (De Genova 2007). Bridget Anderson, Matthew Gibney, and Emanuela Paoletti discuss the deportation of "foreigners" as "a membership-defining act" dedicated to asserting the value and significance of citizenship, and reinforcing the distinction between citizens and non-citizens in terms of the citizenry's "(unconditional) right to residence in the state" (2013:2). Thus, what is ultimately the defining condition of migrants' non-citizenship – their deportability, their susceptibility to deportation – turns out likewise to be a decisive and defining predicate, in the negative, of citizenship itself. Non-deportability is virtually universally upheld to be a principle of modern citizenship. However, this working understanding of citizenship implies a liberal leap of faith that seems to disregard the fullest (illiberal) extent of acts of sovereignty within the toolkit of liberal statecraft that have variously served to constitute and regulate citizenship. We need only be reminded of various historical examples of statutes for the denaturalization (and exclusion) of "undesirable" (or "enemy") citizens, which range from the mundane disqualification of women from their birthright citizenship for marrying "alien" men (Bredbenner 1998) through to the mass de-nationalization an deportation of German citizens – Jews, communists, homosexuals, Gypsies, and so on – to Nazi prison labour camps, and finally, to their extermination (Agamben 1995/1998: 126-35, 166-80). Nonetheless, whereas deportability is indeed conventionally confined to non-citizens, detainability – the susceptibility to detention – is a condition that widely (and perhaps increasingly) also pertains to citizens. In the context of an escalation over recent years in exceptional police measures under the rubric of "security" as well as securitarian law-making, the increasing use in many countries of detention (rather than incarceration), particularly as a purportedly "preventative" measure, confirms that detainability operates as a significantly more general mode of governance than deportability. Thus, much of what I will argue with specific regard to *migrant* detention and detainability has considerably wider ramifications, and often pertains, albeit unevenly, to various categories of citizens as well as non-citizens. The unequal distribution of detention and detainability is a graduated and differential one that not only sorts and ranks according to the inequalities of citizenship status, therefore, but also class inequalities and racialized hierarchies associated with the ascriptive identities of minoritized communities (most notably, Muslim "minorities," citizen and non-citizen alike, in the context of the so-called War on Terror) (cf. De Genova 2007; Eckert 2014). Hereafter, however, I will be restricting the scope of my discussion more exclusively to the detention and detainability of non-citizens.

Detention has indeed become an ever increasingly significant feature of how states govern migration, and consequently, also how they discipline migrants. Hence, this essay is interested in developing the idea of an *economy of detainability*. Again, this concept of "economy" does not refer in any narrow or simple sense to "economics," conventionally understood, although it plainly has implications for how migrants come to be exploited as labor or otherwise are subject to specific types of political or juridical inequalities in the field of activities that we customarily call "the economy." Instead, adapting the Foucauldean conception of an "economy of power," we are interested here in how a wider social field encompassing both "economics" and "politics" involves an unequal distribution of rationalities, techniques and technologies that make migrants subject to detention, and thereby administers and governs them through that uneven distribution of their *detainability*, their greater or lesser susceptibility to detention. All may be more or less susceptible to detention, given particular contingencies and circumstances; some may be detained while many others are not; many may be detained as a prelude to deportation, while still others may be detained and then released, while remaining subject to the prospect of subsequent detentions; others may be detained repeatedly. This is what we may understand by an economy of detainability.

Administrative / Punitive

Detention, like deportation, is a term that has no distinguished pedigree in the history of political ideas and legal concepts. In striking contrast with citizenship, for instance, which derives from a hallowed history of philosophical debate and political practice concerned with the proper relationship of individuals to the public life of a larger community – and again, very much like deportation – detention has no such exalted genealogy. As a figure of law making and law enforcement, of course, actual practices and procedures of detention will always be found to have a history. But there is something distinctly nondescript about the term, perfunctory even, which underscores its status as a kind of understated, largely unexamined fixture of statecraft. To be *detained*, after all, is suggestive of merely being slowed down ("held up"), and is conventionally used in a manner that would suggest that the condition of being detained arises inadvertently, without having been deliberately perpetrated by any active agent. Etymologically, the word's origins would indicate a holding back, or a holding away. Hence, detention is figured as a condition of being "held" in custody, but commonly in a manner that has no strict juridical status, and thus without recourse to the formalities of any due process of law: no actual charges leveled, evidence presented, or legal "rights" stipulated.

Notably, like deportation, detention is pervasively institutionalized as a merely *administrative* measure. Without the formal safeguards customarily built into criminal law, the people subjected to these measures find themselves within the purview of a juridical regime (immigration law) that provides no such protections for its "targets." And yet, detention in its most basic outline involves a coercive deprivation of a person's most elementary liberties. Consequently, something that can only be experienced by the person subjected to it as a profoundly punitive iniquity is presented as an utterly routine and mundane recourse of states "holding" (and eventually, disposing of) their ostensibly unwanted, undesirable, unwelcome foreigners (Dow 2004; Hall 2012; Hasselberg 2016; Welch 2002). By appearing thus to be something that comes about automatically as a mere effect of a seemingly objective condition related to one or another immigration-related "offense," detention (like deportation) comes to appear like an inevitable "fact of life": that is to say, detention tends to be *naturalized*, and rendered more or less unquestionable as a simple and inevitable reality that derives from some sort of self-evident "violation" of the law.

Within the asphyxiating constrictions of such banal language to describe what can only be experienced in fact as a rather punitive if not violent deprivation of very fundamental freedoms, however, we begin to appreciate that with detention – again, very much like deportation – we are in the midst of what Hannah Arendt famously designated as "the banality of evil" (1963). As is well known, Arendt invoked this notion with regard to the unsettling (and terrifying) "normal"-ness of the high-profile Nazi technocrat Adolf Eichmann, during his trial for war crimes, crimes against the Jewish people, and crimes against humanity (1963/2006:276). While Eichmann was widely considered to be directly implicated in the perpetration of a truly extraordinary evil, in other words, Arendt nevertheless discerned something profoundly important about how mundane that evil was when embodied in the non-descript personality of Eichmann. The particular banality of Eichmann's evil derived from what Arendt deemed to be not only "the essence of totalitarian government" but also "perhaps the nature of every bureaucracy": the dehumanizing reduction of individuals into "functionaries and mere cogs in the administrative machinery" (289). It is in this respect that the idea of the "banality of evil" is instructive when we confront and seek to challenge such otherwise routine "administrative" punishments as detention and deportation. The bureaucratic rationality that coldly executes such severely punitive measures as "standard operating procedure," and the consequently heartless disregard for their veritable cruelty for those whose lives are thereby derailed, convert a systemic evil into the simple and banal functionality of a presumptively efficient governmental apparatus.

Arguably even more than the onerous punitive power of deportation itself, detention may be understood to enact the sovereign power of a state upon the lives of migrants in a manner that frequently transmutes their deportable status into a de facto legal non-personhood. That is to say, with detention, the effectively rightless condition of deportable migrants culminates in summary (and sometimes indefinite) incarceration on the basis of little more than their sheer existential predicament as "undesirable" non-citizens, usually with little or no recourse to any form of legal remedy or appeal, and frequently no semblance to any due process of law whatsoever. Migrants subjected to detention, very commonly, are literally "guilty" of nothing other than their "unauthorized" (illegalized) status, penalized simply for being who and what they are, and not at all for any act of wrong-doing. With detention, nonetheless, they are subjected to a condition of direct confinement by state authorities, often castigated to a station effectively *outside the law*, and thereby rendered veritably rightless – sometimes indefinitely. This proposition should not be understood to be universal or absolute, of course. To speak of such a condition – not only outside of the purview and protections of criminal law but even beyond the reach of other administrative bodies of law, such as immigration law – we are indeed speaking of migrant detention in pronouncedly illiberal political contexts, not uncommonly characterized by high levels of impunity, and plagued by severe deprivation and outright cruelty, including physical abuse and torture. Yet even in putatively liberal political contexts, such as the United States, there is no dearth of evidence to confirm the rather appallingly high degree of administrative "lawlessness" and sheer brutality that prevails in both conventional policing and incarceration, as well as migrant detention (cf. Burridge et al. 2012; Dow 2004; Garland 2001; Gilmore 2007; Gottschalk 2006; James 2000; 2007; Price 2015; Simon 2007; Wacquant 2009). Furthermore, during recent years, in many countries, there has also been an alarming conflation of criminal and immigration law – "crimmigration" (Stumpf 2006) – which has aggressively contributed to the outright criminalization of various forms of migrant "illegality" and the subsumption of immigration-related "offenses" within the purview of actual criminal law, prompting new avenues of critical inquiry into the concept of governing migration through crime (Dowling and Inda 2013).

In any case, the indeterminacy that prevails in migrant detention, even within relatively liberal juridical regimes, inflicts a subtle and unfathomable cruelty upon those detained. For many migrants subjected to detention, consequently, deportation at least represents the comparative relief of knowing that the punitive process will end once the expulsion has been accomplished, at which point they may then be relatively free to resume some semblance of normal life, albeit back "home" in the country from which they previously departed. Of course, for some migrants or refugees, deportation only delivers them back into the hands of authorities in their ostensible "home" countries, where they may be "detained" or imprisoned anew, and sometimes also subjected to torture (see, e.g. Bhartia 2010; Kanstroom 2012). Likewise, even for those deportees who are indeed "free" to resume their lives following their coercive return "home," life is often unviable (see, e.g. Coutin 2010; Kanstroom 2012; Peutz 2010). Nonetheless, detention – being "held in custody," in contrast to being "sent back" somewhere and presumably released – often involves imprisonment aggravated by excruciating uncertainty and indeterminacy about any future prospect of release. Little surprise, then, that many detainees would prefer to be deported immediately rather than remain stuck in detention. In other instances, after having served a prison sentence for a conviction for an ordinary criminal offense, migrants (including long-term "legal" residents) abruptly discover that – for no other reason than the mere fact of their statutory non-citizenship – they must suffer the double punishment of expulsion: upon completion of their prison terms, they are summarily delivered into detention (sometimes indefinite) and informed, frequently to their utter shock, that they will be deported as "criminal aliens" (cf. Griffiths 2015; Hasselberg 2016; Kanstroom 2012). In either case, being "detained" introduces a panoply of both legal ambiguities and existential uncertainties for non-citizens that commonly far exceed and casually dispense with the juridical parameters otherwise afforded to ordinary "criminal" citizens who have been incarcerated for conventional convictions.

Indistinction / Indeterminacy

Thus, their detention frequently leaves non-citizens at the mercy of the caprices of the immediate enforcers of their confinement. Here, we may be instructively reminded of Giorgio Agamben's crucial insight that "the police" – and we may add here, also prison guards or other similarly immediate enforcers of order within detention facilities – "are not merely an administrative function of law enforcement; rather, the police are perhaps the place where the proximity and the almost constitutive exchange between violence and right that characterizes the figure of the sovereign is shown more nakedly and clearly than anywhere else" (1996/2000:103). That is to say, in Agamben's account, the sovereign power of the modern (liberal, constitutional, democratic) state significantly derives from the capacity to decide upon when there exists a "state of exception" (Agamben 2003), or a "state of emergency," that requires the state to disregard or suspend the law in order to putatively preserve the integrity of the larger political and juridical order that relies on the Rule of Law. Thus, there inevitably exists what Agamben calls a "zone of indistinction," which is to say, an area of ambiguity, where it is possible to suspend the separation of "right" (the law, as an abstraction, that appears to delimit the state's exercise of power over its subjects) from brute force (the sheer fact of perpetrating violence to enforce relations of rule or domination). If this is so, then the police (and the detention or prison guards) similarly operate on a continuous everyday basis at the blurry intersection where the abstract universality of "the law" routinely becomes real only through the immediate, concrete, interpersonal coercive or violent encounter where "the law" in general is applied, or enacted, in specific instances through its enforcement. Thus, the lowest-level enforcers of the law must constantly exercise their own discretion and routinely decide on a case-by-case basis on the "state of exception" between the abstraction of the law and the fact of violence that enforces it, in the putative interests of "order" or "security." In this sense, it is not necessary for the state to proclaim a "state of emergency" or "martial law" to see that sovereignty is permanently derived from the sorts of acts of "law enforcement" that involve the discretionary exercise of power (including violent coercion) by the most low-level enforcers of "order." For these ordinary police and prison or detention authorities, the law, in its abstraction and generality, remains largely silent about how it must be applied and enforced through greater or lesser acts of violence. Such mundane acts of enforcement are largely authorized by the law, and yet operate outside of strict purview of the law, and depend on the discretion and predilections of those who embody the state's sovereign power in the "zone of indistinction" that is everyday life.

Migrant detention often is imposed as a prelude to eventual deportation, although it is also common that actual deportation is not possible for various reasons and consequently, detained migrants are repeatedly released after periods of more or less prolonged interruption of their ordinary lives. Hence, whereas deportation must be situated alongside a variety of other practices of expulsion and in this way represents a kind of coercive *mobility*, or forced movement (Walters 2002), detention instead signals a practice of confinement, and therefore coercive *immobilization*. Notably, detention appears within the purview of "human rights" as a rather generic figure of imprisonment. Article 9 of the Universal Declaration of Human Rights states: "No one shall be subjected to arbitrary arrest, detention or exile." In this regard, detention and imprisonment are effectively synonymous. Hence, detention must be situated within the nexus of diverse forms of captivity and confinement (Foucault 1972-73/2015; 1975/1979; cf. Walters 2004:248). Nonetheless, while located within this continuum of coercive confinement, detention must be also distinguished from other forms of incarceration. What chiefly characterizes detention as such is the extent to which it has been reserved as a category for naming precisely those varieties of confinement that are intended to be emphatically distinguished from the more customarily juridical coordinates of penal imprisonment for criminal offenses. In short, detainees are so designated precisely because they are understood to *not* be "prisoners"; detention is so named exactly to the extent that it is conceived to be something that is *not* incarceration. Here, indeed, we may recall Arendt's memorable insight into the cruel and revealing irony that common criminals in fact had more legal rights and recognition than those "interned" in the Nazi concentration camps, or indeed, than those relegated to the status of stateless refugees (1951/1968:286). To be a "criminal" is to be subjected to the recriminations of the law, and thus to be inscribed within the law and its punishments; in contrast, to be a detainee is to be subjected to an "administrative" apparatus, and as a consequence, to potentially (not always, but not uncommonly) be figured as effectively outside of the purview of the law altogether.

Ensnared within the pompous gestures of "national" sovereignty and a state's prerogative to enforce its own (bordered) legal order, therefore, the detention of non-citizens – a punishment that is activated often for no other reason than a person's mere status as an "irregular" non-citizen – underscores the more elementary fact that some people's lives are plainly judged to be *unworthy of justice*. More specifically, non-citizens – for no other reason that their pure identity as such – may always be (at least, potentially) relegated to a de facto status of juridical non-personhood: hence, the often arbitrary and authoritarian character of detention regimes.

Time / Discipline

The detention power commonly operates outside and beyond the parameters of any system of criminal law, and has ordinarily been figured as merely a matter of expediency in a state's presumed eventual disposal (deportation) of illegalized or criminalized migrants. To adequately comprehend the productivity of this power to detain migrants, we therefore need recourse to a concept of *detainability*: the susceptibility to detention, the possibility of being detained (De Genova 2007). Just as deportability is much more about the deep consequentiality of the possibility of being deported even if most remain un-deported (De Genova 2002; 2005:213-50; 2010b), then, detainability (the susceptibility to being detained) – and also actual detentions that do not culminate in deportation – serve to *discipline* migrants' lives through the unfathomable interruptions that exacerbate their precarity. Thus, we must interrogate the economy of different conditionalities and diverse contingencies (Goldring and Landolt 2013) – within historically specific regimes of immigration, asylum, and citizenship – that undergird the various degrees by which distinct categories of migrants are subjected to this susceptibility to the detention power. Such an economy of detainablility always necessarily implies that some non-citizens are more susceptible than others to the punitive recriminations of any given detention regime, and experience their relative vulnerability to detention (their detainability) unequally, within a nexus of different degrees of precarity for those whom it subjects to its power (De Genova 2007; see, e.g. Griffiths 2015; Hasselberg 2016).

A non-citizen's susceptibility to detention – her detainability – therefore involves a deeply existential predicament that is defined by the grim prospect of being apprehended and coercively removed from the spaces and temporalities of everyday life. In this respect, detention provides an instructive example of what Agamben (1995/1998:175) designates "dislocating localization": people are forcibly dislocated form their lives but nonetheless coercively held in a particular place. Plainly, this term could likewise describe ordinary imprisonment. For present purposes, it is instructive to underscore that spatial confinement and captivity is also an interruption of the detainees' *time*. Indeed, detention always entails the enforcement of a dire and usually abrupt separation of an individual non-citizen from all the material and practical coordinates of her day-to-day circumstances, the actual life and livelihood that she has been engaged in sustaining and cultivating, as well as all the immediate and affective human relationships of which these are made. Even if the end result is only that migrants are released when actual deportation has proven to be unfeasible, the rhythms of their lives and their larger life projects are profoundly fractured (sometimes repeatedly) by coercive periods of detention. In this respect, detainability is as much entangled (and sometimes even more so) with a migrant's actual *un*-deportability as with her actionable deportability (the prospect of actual deportation). While all of the foregoing is also true of ordinary incarceration, the excruciating difference commonly at stake in detention is the deeply ambiguous and profoundly punitive dimension of *temporal* indeterminacy. In *The Punitive Society*, Michel Foucault remarkably examines the profound correspondence of "the prison-form of penalty" and the "the wage-form of labor" (1972-73/2015:261) as "historically twin forms" (71), predicated upon "the introduction of the quantity of time as measure, and not only as economic measure ... but also as moral measure" (83), and hence, "the introduction of *time* into the capitalist system of power and into the system of penalty," whereby "the time of life" is "exchanged against power" (72; emphasis in original). In short, the prison-form of penalty presupposes a strict quantification of (life-)time – as measure – that is, in effect, exchanged according to a rational calculus. In striking contrast, detention – and the uncertain prospect of eventual deportation, as well as the uncertain prospect of non-deportation and release, shadowed by the prospect of subsequent detention – delivers the detainable non-citizen into a quintessentially Kafkaesque nightmare (cf. Bhartia 2010; Cohen 2016; van Houtum 2010).

Nevertheless, detainability persists as a fundamentally (if diffused) disciplinary mechanism of social control and domination. Like the ominous prospect of deportation, then, the always unpredictable possibility of detention becomes a defining horizon for many migrants' experience of everyday life. This prospective risk of detention, furthermore, enforces a protracted condition of vulnerability to the recriminations of the law, and consequently, a complex and variegated spectrum of ways in which everyday life becomes riddled with precarity, multiple conditionalities, inequality, and uncertainty. In this respect, detainability is also a *temporal* predicament that can render one's way of life and one's life projects to be always relatively tentative and tenuous (Coutin 2000:27-47). Detainability, like deportability, is therefore entangled with a protracted socio-political condition of uncertainty and the lived precarity that ensues from the unpredictable hazard of apprehension and detention.

Hence, the detention power capitalizes on the amorphous temporalities of indefinite (possibly perpetual) *waiting*.[2] As Pierre Bourdieu notes:

> "Absolute power is the power to make oneself unpredictable and deny other people any reasonable anticipation, to place them in total uncertainty.... The all-powerful is he who does not wait but who makes others wait.... Waiting implies submission.... It follows that the art of 'taking one's time' ... of making people wait ... is an integral part of the exercise of power..." (1997/2000:228).

Vexed with precautions and often overshadowed by a diffuse but persistent terror – the fear of detection, arrest, detention, and deportation – those who are subjected to the prospect of detention are subjected to a banal (pseudo-)"administrative" power that in fact conceals a brute authoritarianism. This seemingly mundane and merely bureaucratic condition invariably reveals its absolutist character by enforcing a condition of indefinite waiting and being made to live with protracted uncertainty – even if it is never activated in the form of an actual detention. Yet, these more or less torturous conditions of life for those who are compelled by circumstances to make their lives beneath the horizon of the possibility of detention have been made ever increasingly normal -- "terribly and terrifyingly normal" (to recall Arendt's phrase) -- within our modern global detention and deportation regime.

---

2 There is a growing literature – primarily ethnographic in character, and with a noteworthy prominence of studies concerned with migration – on the phenomenology and socio-political consequentiality of "waiting"; see Anderson et al. (2013); Andersson (2014a,b); Auyero (2012); Bear (2014); Bredeloup (2012); Coutin (2003; 2005); Crapanzano (1985); Cwerner (2001); Griffiths (2014); Hage (2009); Hall (2012); Hasselberg (2016) Jeffrey (2010); Khosravi (2009; 2014); Mountz (2011); Mountz et al. (2002); Repak (1995); Schwartz (1974; 1975); Sutton et al. (2011); van Houtum (2010). Likewise, there are important precursors to this incipient field of inquiry within more theoretically informed Marxian and feminist studies of the temporalities of social reproduction; see Adam (2002; 2008); Baraitser (2014); Bryon (2007) Castree (2009); Conlon (2011); Edensor (2006); Harvey (1990); Lefebvre 1994; Massey 1992; Thompson (1967).

Bibliography

Adam, Barbara. 2002. "The Gendered Time Politics of Globalisation: Of Shadowlands and Elusive Justice." *Feminist Review* 70: 3-29.

Adam, Barbara. 2008. "Of Timespaces, Futurescapes and Timeprints" (Lüneburg University, 17 June 2008); available at: <http://www.cardiff.ac.uk/socsi/futures/conf_ba_lueneberg170608.pdf>.

Agamben, Giorgio. 1995/1998. *Homo Sacer: Sovereign Power and Bare Life*. Stanford, CA: Stanford University Press.

Agamben, Giorgio. 1996/2000. *Means without End: Notes on Politics*. Minneapolis: University of Minnesota Press.

Agamben, Giorgio. 2003/2005. *State of Exception*. Chicago: University of Chicago Press.

Anderson, Bridget; Matthew Gibney, and Emanuela Paoletti, eds. 2013. *The Social, Political and Historical Contours of Deportation*. New York & London: Springer.

Andersson, Ruben. 2014a. *Illegality, Inc.: Clandestine Migration and the Business of Bordering Europe*. Berkeley: University of California Press.

Andersson, Ruben. 2014b. "Time and the Migrant Other: European Border Controls and the Temporal Economics of Illegality." *American Anthropologist* 116(4): 795-809.

Arendt, Hannah. 1951/1968. *The Origins of Totalitarianism*. New York: Harvest/Harcourt.

Arendt, Hannah. 1963/2006. *Eichmann in Jerusalem: A Report on the Banality of Evil*. New York: Penguin.

Auyero, Javier. 2012. *Patients of the State: The Politics of Waiting in Argentina*. Durham: Duke University Press.

Baraitser, L. 2014. "Time and Again: Repetition, Maternity and the Non-Reproductive." *Studies in the Maternal* 6(1), www.mamsie.bbk.ac.uk

Bear, L. 2014. "Doubt, Conflict, Mediation: The Anthropology of Modern Time." *JRAI*

Bhartia, Aashti. 2010. "Fictions of Law: The Trial of Sulaiman Oladokun, or Reading Kafka in an Immigration Court." In: Nicholas De Genova and Nathalie Peutz, eds, *The Deportation Regime: Sovereignty, Space, and the Freedom of Movement*. Durham, NC: Duke University Press: 329–50

Bredbenner, Candice Lewis. 1998. *A Nationality of Her Own: Women, Marriage and the Law of Citizenship*. Berkeley: University of California Press.

Bredeloup, Sylvie. 2012. "Sahara Transit: Times, Spaces, Places." *Population, Space and Place* 18: 457-467.
Bourdieu, Pierre. 1997/2000. *Pascalian Meditations*. Stanford, CA: Stanford University Press.
Bryon, Valerie. 2007. *Gender and the Politics of Time: Feminist Theory and Contemporary Debates*. Bristol: Polity Press.
Burridge, Andrew, Jenna Loyd, and Matthew Mitchelson, eds. 2012. *Beyond Walls and Cages: Prisons, Borders, and Global Crisis*. Athens: University of Georgia Press.
Castree, Noel. 2009. "The Spatio-Temporality of Capitalism." *Time & Society* 18(1): 26-61.
Chauvin, Sébastien and Blanca Garcés-Mascareñas. 2012. "Beyond Informal Citizenship: The New Moral Economy of Migrant Illegality." *International Political Sociology* 6(3): 241-59.
Cohen, Roger. 2016. "Broken Men in Paradise: The world's refugee crisis knows no more sinister exercise in cruelty than Australia's island prisons." *New York Times Opinion* (9 December 2016). Available at: http://www.nytimes.com/2016/12/09/opinion/sunday/australia-refugee-prisons-manus-island.html
Conlon, Deirdre. 2011. "Waiting: Feminist Perspectives on the Spacings/Timings of Migrant (Im)Mobility." *Gender, Place & Culture* 18(3), 353-360.
Coutin, Susan Bibler. 2003. *Legalizing Moves: Salvadoran Immigrants' Struggle for U.S. Residency*. Ann Arbor: University of Michigan Press.
Coutin, Susan Bibler. 2005. "Being en Route." *American Anthropologist* 107(2): 195-206.
Coutin, Susan Bibler. 2010. "Exiled by Law: Deportation and the Inviability of Life." In: Nicholas De Genova and Nathalie Peutz, eds, *The Deportation Regime: Sovereignty, Space, and the Freedom of Movement*. Durham, NC: Duke University Press: 351–70.
Crapanzano, Vincent. 1985. *Waiting: The Whites of South Africa*. London: Granada.
Cwerner, Saulo B. 2001. "The Times of Migration." *Journal of Ethnic and Migration Studies* 27(1): 7–36.
De Genova, Nicholas. 2002. "Migrant 'Illegality' and Deportability in Everyday Life." *Annual Review of Anthropology* 31: 419-47.
De Genova, Nicholas. 2005. *Working the Boundaries: Race, Space, and "Illegality" in Mexican Chicago*. Durham, NC: Duke University Press.

De Genova, Nicholas. 2007. "The Production of Culprits: From Deportability to Detainability in the Aftermath of 'Homeland Security'." *Citizenship Studies* 11(5): 421-48.

De Genova, Nicholas. 2010a. "Antiterrorism, Race, and the New Frontier: American Exceptionalism, Imperial Multiculturalism, and the Global Security State." *Identities* 17(6): 613-640.

De Genova, Nicholas. 2010b. "The Deportation Regime: Sovereignty, Space, and the Freedom of Movement." Theoretical Overview. In: Nicholas De Genova and Nathalie Peutz, eds, *The Deportation Regime: Sovereignty, Space, and the Freedom of Movement*. Durham, NC: Duke University Press: 33–65.

De Genova, Nicholas. 2013. "Spectacles of Migrant 'Illegality': The Scene of Exclusion, the Obscene of Inclusion." *Ethnic and Racial Studies* 36(7): 1180-98.

De Genova, Nicholas. 2014. "Deportation." In Bridget Anderson and Michael Keith, eds, *Migration: A COMPAS Anthology*. Centre on Migration, Policy and Society (COMPAS), Oxford: Oxford University Press; available at: <http://compasanthology.co.uk>.

De Genova, Nicholas. 2015a. "Extremities and Regularities: Regulatory Regimes and the Spectacle of Immigration Enforcement." In: Yolande Jansen, Robin Celikates, and Joost de Bloois, eds, *The Irregularisation of Migration in Contemporary Europe: Detention, Deportation, Drowning*. London: Rowman & Littlefield: 3–14.

De Genova, Nicholas and Nathalie Peutz, eds. 2010. *The Deportation Regime: Sovereignty, Space, and the Freedom of Movement*. Durham, NC: Duke University Press.

Dow, Mark. 2004. *American Gulag: Inside U.S. Immigration Prisons*. Berkeley: University of California Press.

Dowling, Julie A. and Jonathan Xavier Inda, eds. 2013. *Governing Immigration Through Crime: A Reader*. Stanford, CA: Stanford University Press.

Eckert, Julia. 2014. "Preventive Laws and the Policing of the Urban Poor." In: Nandini Gooptu and Jonathan Parry, eds, *The Persistence of Poverty in India*. New Delhi: Social Science Press: 291–316.

Edensor, Tim. 2006. "Reconsidering National Temporalities: Institutional Times, Everyday Routines, Serial Spaces and Synchronicities." *European Journal of Social Theory* 9(4): 525-545.

Foucault, Michel. 1972-73/2015. *The Punitive Society: Lectures at the Collège de France, 1972-1973*. Basingstoke, UK: Palgrave Macmillan.
Foucault, Michel.1975/1979. *Discipline and Punish: The Birth of the Prison*. New York: Random House.
Garland, David. 2001. *The Culture of Control: Crime and Social Order in Contemporary Society*. New York: Oxford University Press.
Gilmore, Ruth W. 2007. *Golden Gulag: Prisons, Surplus, Crisis, and Opposition in Globalizing California*. Berkeley: University of California Press.
Goldring, Luin and Patricia Landolt. 2013. "The Conditionality of Legal Status and Rights: Conceptualizing Precarious Non-Citizenship in Canada." In: Luin Goldring and Patricia Landolt, eds, *Producing and Negotiating Non-citizenship: Precarious Legal Status in Canada*. Toronto: University of Toronto Press: 3–30.
Gottschalk, Marie. 2006. *The Prison and the Gallows: The Politics of Mass Incarceration in America*. New York: Cambridge University Press.
Griffiths, Melanie B. 2014. "Out of Time: The Temporal Uncertainties of Refused Asylum Seekers and Immigration Detainees." *Journal of Ethnic and Migration Studies* 40(12): 1991-2009.
Griffiths, Melanie B. 2015. "The Convergence of the Criminal and the Foreigner in the Production of Citizenship." In: Bridget Anderson and Vanessa Hughes, eds, *Citizenship and its Others*. Basingstoke, UK: Palgrave Macmillan: 72–88.
Griffiths, Melanie B., Ali Rogers, and Bridget Anderson. 2013. "Migration, Time and Temporalities: Review and Prospect." *COMPAS Research Resources Paper. Centre on Migration, Policy and Society (COMPAS)*, Oxford: COMPAS.
Hage, Ghassan. 2009. "Waiting Out the Crisis: On Stuckedness and Governmentality." In: Ghassan Hage, ed., *Waiting*. Carlton: Melbourne University Press: 97–106.
Hall, Alexandra. 2012. *Border Watch: Cultures of Immigration, Detention and Control*. London: Pluto Press.
Harvey, David. 1990. *The Condition of Postmodernity: An Enquiry into the Origins of Cultural Change*. Malden, MA: Blackwell.
Hasselberg, Ines. 2016. *Enduring Uncertainty: Deportation, Punishment and Everyday Life*. Oxford: Berghahn Books.
James, Joy, ed. 2000. *States of Confinement: Policing, Detention, and Prisons*. New York: St. Martin's Press.

James, Joy, ed. 2007. *Warfare in the American Homeland: Policing and Prison in a Penal Democracy*. Durham, NC: Duke University Press.

Jeffrey, Craig. 2010. *Timepass: Youth, Class, and the Politics of Waiting in India*. Stanford, CA: Stanford University Press.

Kanstroom, Daniel. 2012. *Aftermath: Deportation Law and the New American Diaspora*. New York, Oxford University Press.

Khosravi, Shahram. 2009. "Detention and Deportation of Asylum Seekers in Sweden." *Race & Class* 50(4): 38-56.

Khosravi, Shahram. 2014. "Waiting." In: Bridget Anderson and Michael Keith, eds, *Migration: A COMPAS Anthology. Centre on Migration, Policy and Society (COMPAS)*, Oxford: Oxford University Press.

Lefebvre, Henri. 1994/2013. *Rhythmanalysis: Space, Time and Everyday Life*. London: Bloomsbury.

Massey, Doreen. 1992. "Politics and Space/Time." *New Left Review* 196

Mountz, Alison. 2011. "Where Asylum-Seekers Wait: Feminist Counter-Topographies of Sites between States." *Gender, Place & Culture* 18(3): 381–399.

Mountz, Alison, R. Wright, I. Miyares, and A.J. Bailey. 2002. "Lives in Limbo: Temporary Protected Status and Immigrant Identities." *Global Networks* 2(4): 335-356.

Peutz, Nathalie. 2010. "'Criminal Alien' Deportees in Somaliland: An Ethnography of Removal." In: Nicholas De Genova and Nathalie Peutz, eds, *The Deportation Regime: Sovereignty, Space, and the Freedom of Movement*. Durham, NC: Duke University Press: 371–411.

Price, Joshua M. 2015. *Prison and Social Death*. New Brunswick, NJ: Rutgers University Press.

Repak, Terry. 1995. *Waiting on Washington: Central American Workers in the Nation's Capital*. Philadelphia: Temple University Press.

Schwartz, Barry. 1974. "Waiting, Exchange, and Power: The Distribution of Time in Social Systems." *American Journal of Sociology* 79: 841–870.

Schwartz, Barry. 1975. *Queuing and Waiting*. Chicago: University of Chicago Press.

Simon, Jonathan. 2007. *Governing Through Crime: How the War on Crime Transformed American Democracy and Created a Culture of Fear*. New York: Oxford University Press.

Stumpf, Juliet P. 2006. "The Crimmigration Crisis: Immigrants, Crime, and Sovereign Power." *American University Law Review* 56: 367-419.

Sutton, Rebecca, Darshan Vigneswaran, and Harry Wels. 2011. "Waiting in Liminal Space: Migrants' Queuing for Home Affairs in South Africa." *Anthropology Southern Africa* 34(1&2): 30–37.
Thompson, E.P. 1967. "Time, Work-Discipline, and Industrial Capitalism." *Past & Present* 38.
van Houtum, Henk. 2010. "Waiting Before the Law: Kafka on the Border." *Social & Legal Studies* 19(3): 285–297.
Walters, William. 2002. "Deportation, Expulsion and the International Police of Aliens." Citizenship Studies 6(3): 265-292. Reprinted in Nicholas De Genova and Nathalie Peutz, eds, *The Deportation Regime: Sovereignty, Space, and the Freedom of Movement*. Durham, NC: Duke University Press (2010): 69–100.
Walters, William. 2004. "Secure Borders, Safe Haven, Domopolitics." *Citizenship Studies* 8(3): 237-60.
Wacquant, Loïc. 2009. *Punishing the Poor: The Neoliberal Government of Social Insecurity*. Durham NC: Duke University Press.
Welch, Michael. 2002. *Detained: Immigration Laws and the Expanding I.N.S. Jail Complex*. Philadelphia: Temple University Press.
Welch, Michael and Liza Schuster. 2005. "Detention of Asylum Seekers in the US, UK, France, Germany and Italy: A Critical View of the Globalizing Culture of Control." *Criminal Justice* 5(4): 331–55.

Authors

Laura Affolter is a postdoctoral researcher at the Hamburg Institute for Social Research. She obtained her PhD from the University of Bern in 2017. In her dissertation, she examined everyday practices of decision-making in the Swiss Secretariat for Migration. She thereby focused on the regularities of asylum decision-making: on the shaping of patterns of practice and on decision-makers' institutional socialisation. In her current research project, 'Using the Constitution against the State: The Rights of Nature and Struggles over Industrial Mining in Ecuador', she examines constitutional lawsuits brought against (planned) mining projects in Ecuador and the mobilisation of the Rights of Nature in these legal struggles. Laura Affolter is co-editor of Tsantsa.

Simon Affolter is a member of the academic staff at the Centre for Democracy Studies Aarau (Switzerland), doing research on education in the migration society. He obtained his PhD in Social Anthropology from the University of Bern in 2018. For his dissertation he did research on seasonal labour migrants in the agricultural industry in the midlands of Switzerland. The dissertation analyses the influence of the differentiated border regime on the working and living conditions of migrants.

Nicholas De Genova (www.nicholasdegenova.com) is Professor and Chair of the Department of Comparative Cultural Studies at the University of Houston. He previously held teaching appointments in urban and political geography at King's College London, and in anthropology at Stanford, Columbia, and Goldsmiths, University of London, as well as visiting professorships or research positions at the Universities of Warwick, Bern, and Amsterdam. He is the author of *Working the Boundaries: Race, Space, and "Illegality" in Mexican Chicago* (2005), co-author of *Latino Crossings: Mexicans, Puerto Ricans,* *and the Politics of Race and Citizenship* (2003), editor of *Racial Transformations: Latinos and Asians Remaking the United States* (2006), co-editor of *The Deportation Regime: Sovereignty, Space, and the Freedom of Movement* (2010), editor of *The Borders of "Europe": Autonomy of Migration, Tactics of Bordering* (2017), and co-editor of *Roma Migrants in the European Union: Un/Free Mobility* (2019).

Julia Eckert is Professor for Political Anthropology at the University of Bern, Switzerland. She has a research focus in legal anthropology, the anthropology of the state, and social movements. In her current research she explores the relation between moral and legal norms and the changes in institutions of responsibility, participation and redistribution. Before joining the University of Bern, she was head of the research group 'Law against the State' at the Max Planck Institute for Social Anthropology, Halle/Saale which examined the juridification of protest and the transnationalisation of legal norms. She has worked on Hindu-nationalist movements, the police and security legislation in India, and on legal reform in Uzbekistan and Afghanistan. Her publications include: The Charisma of Direct Action (Oxford University Press 2003); The Social Life of Anti-Terrorism Laws (Transcript 2008); Law against the State (Cambridge University Press 2012). She is co-editor of Anthropological Theory.

David Loher is a postdoctoral researcher and lecturer at the Institute for Social Anthropology in Bern, from where he received his PhD. In his dissertation «The Limits of Control» (University of Bern 2016), he examined the interdependencies between transnational migration trajectories of young male Tunisian migrants and the emerging migration regime between Tunisia and Switzerland, with a particular focus on the governance of so-called voluntary return. He is interested in questions at the intersection between the anthropology of migration, legal anthropology and the anthropology of the state. His current research focuses on the asbestos industry and the temporal and spatial dimension of the allocation of responsibility in global world society. David Loher is co-editor of Tsantsa.

Chowra Makaremi is Chargée de recherche CNRS, Paris. Her research activity focuses on the anthropology of the State, everyday and legal forms of violence, and processes of subjectivation at the margins. It also reflects on the methods of knowledge production and dissemination. It explores the ethnography of the State in France (migrations, national frontiers and social boundaries), and the ethnography of violence in Iran (post-revolution experiences and legacies). She co-edited several volumes on migration and border control (*Enfermés dehors: le confinement des étrangers en Europe*, Le Croquant 2009; *Le confinement des étrangers: entre circulation et enfermement*, Cultures et Conflits 71(3), 2008). She is the co-author, with Didier Fassin and alii, of *At the Hearth of the State. The Moral World of Institutions*, London, Pluto Press 2015; and the author of the non-fiction *Aziz's Notebook. At the hearth of the Iranian revolution* (Paris, Gallimard, 2011), as well as a graphic novel based on her fieldwork in Paris' border detention centre: *Prisonniers du Passage* (with Matthieu Pehau, Steinkis, 2019). She is the director of the ERC research programme "Off-Site: Violence, State formation and memory politics: an off-site ethnography of post-revolution Iran" (2018-2023).

Werner Schiffauer is Professor em. of Comparative Social and Cultural Anthropology at the European University Viadrina Frankfurt (Oder). His research interests include anthropology of migration, the organization of societal heterogeneity, Islam in Europe and anthropology of the state. Amongst his numerous publications are *Parallelgesellschaften. Wieviel Wertekonsens braucht unsere Gesellschaft? Ethnographische Überlegungen*, Bielefeld: transcript, 2008; *Nach dem Islamismus. Die Islamische Gemeinde Milli Görüş. Eine Ethnographie*, Frankfurt am Main: Suhrkamp, 2010; *Schule, Moschee, Elternhaus. Eine ethnologische Intervention*, Berlin : Suhrkamp, 2015, (Together with Anne Eilert und Marlene Rudloff, eds.); *So schaffen wir das. Eine Zivilgesellschaft im Aufbruch*, Bielefeld: transcript. 2017.

Social Sciences

kollektiv orangotango+ (Ed.)
This Is Not an Atlas
A Global Collection of Counter-Cartographies

2018, 352 p., hardcover, col. ill.
34,99 € (DE), 978-3-8376-4519-4
E-Book: available as free open access publication
E-Book: ISBN 978-3-8394-4519-8

Mozilla Foundation
Internet Health Report 2019

2019, 118 p., pb., ill.
19,99 € (DE), 978-3-8376-4946-8
E-Book: available as free open access publication
E-Book: ISBN 978-3-8394-4946-2

James Martin
Psychopolitics of Speech
Uncivil Discourse and the Excess of Desire

2019, 186 p., hardcover
79,99 € (DE), 978-3-8376-3919-3
E-Book: 79,99 € (DE), ISBN 978-3-8394-3919-7

All print, e-book and open access versions of the titles in our list
are available in our online shop www.transcript-verlag.de/en!

Social Sciences

Michael Bray
Powers of the Mind
Mental and Manual Labor
in the Contemporary Political Crisis

2019, 208 p., hardcover
99,99 € (DE), 978-3-8376-4147-9
E-Book: 99,99 € (DE), ISBN 978-3-8394-4147-3

Iain MacKenzie
Resistance and the Politics of Truth
Foucault, Deleuze, Badiou

2018, 148 p., pb.
29,99 € (DE), 978-3-8376-3907-0
E-Book: 26,99 € (DE), ISBN 978-3-8394-3907-4
EPUB: 26,99 € (DE), ISBN 978-3-7328-3907-0

Alexander Schellinger, Philipp Steinberg (eds.)
The Future of the Eurozone
How to Keep Europe Together:
A Progressive Perspective from Germany

2017, 202 p., pb.
29,99 € (DE), 978-3-8376-4081-6
E-Book: 26,99 € (DE), ISBN 978-3-8394-4081-0
EPUB: 26,99 € (DE), ISBN 978-3-7328-4081-6

**All print, e-book and open access versions of the titles in our list
are available in our online shop www.transcript-verlag.de/en!**